THE MALAY LANGUAGE GUIDE BOOK

For Tourists and Foreign Residents

By

Andrew Tadross
&
Mae Cheong

THE MALAY LANGUAGE GUIDEBOOK

for Tourists and Foreign Residents

Copyright © 2017

Andrew Tadross,

Mae Cheong

All Rights Reserved

ISBN-13: 978-1545324400

ISBN-10: 1545324409

AKNOWLEDGEMENT

Mae Cheong

This book is to be dedicated to my dearest parents, my brother David, my siblings and my two daughters, Ashleigh and Melanie. In addition, the dedication goes to my very good friends, Peter Cheong, Leong Lee See, May Lau, Leong Bee Leng, Janice Hughes, Barry Hughes, Frederik Jourvalenko, Christine Mouyon, Jeya Jayaratnam, Siew Li Yap and Thangathai. Also, to my late paternal grandmother, Madam Foong Kwai Chun, my late buddies, Christina Kok Wai Leng and Brian Wallis.

A special thank you to Andrew Tadross. He had encouraged me to work together in making this book. Thanking my Malay tutor, Puan Rosmah Dahalan, M. Ed.(Sociology), who has assisted and contributed explanations on contextual and grammatical uses of the Malay language in parts of this guide book.

Thanking the contributing artists, Christine Mouyon, Andrew Tadross, Ashleigh Wong and Melanie Wong for their most appreciated paintings and sketches. Also, the cover design contributions by Siew Li Yap and A. Tadross.

Book cover paintings contributed by Christine Mouyon and Andrew Tadross.

Artwork by Andrew Tadross, Ashleigh Wong, Melanie Wong, C. Mouyon and Mae Cheong.

Cover graphics designed by Siew Li Yap and Andrew Tadross

Andrew Tadross

Dedicated to my wonderful late friend, Chrsitina Kok, and her children Siu-lin Siobhan O'brien, Ben Jian-min Porter, and Mei-lin Porter.

Contents

ABOUT THE MALAY LANGUAGE

The Malay language derives from the Austronesian family of dialects and falls into the branch called *Nusantara* which includes several hundred languages. The *Bahasa Melayu* has 24 original sounds, with 18 consonants and six vocals (Tatabahasa Dewan 3rd.Ed).Well positioned for trade, the Malay archipelago has assimilated various cultural influences as well as spread its culture regionally, resulting in the Malay language that has incorporated multiple dialects, derived forms from other languages, and has also evolved over eras.

The national language of Malaysia, is officially the **Malay Language** or *Bahasa Melayu*. The language is spoken by most of the 30 million residents of the nation. Legislation introduced in 1967 (National Language Act) designates the Latin alphabet (called *Rumi* in Malay) as the official script of the national language.   The traditional Malay script had used the *Jawi* script. Standardization of the Malay spelling systems were organized with Indonesia in 1972 through the Indonesian-Malay Language Council (Majlis Bahasa Indonesia-Malaysia, MBIM) and also the Brunei Languuage Council as a regional collaboration in the management of the languages' spelling standardization (Tatabahasa Dewan 3rd.Ed).

Historical influences on the Malay language came from Arabic, Persian and Sanskrit, during the "golden age" of Islam in Southeast Asia. Words derived from Arabic include **Q'uran**, **ilmiah** (knowledge), **hadir** (present), **syaitan** (devil).   Modern influences on the Malay language come from Greek, Latin and English, through numerous cognates, mainly words relating to science, technology and global culture (internet, wifi, antiobiotic, hip-hop, etc).   Malay has incorporated many words and phrases with Chinese roots from the *Straits Chinese* (the Baba Nyonya / Peranakan) during the Malaccan Sultanate era, such as **sepatu** (*shoes*), **pantang** (*superstitious*), **tahan** (*tolerate*), **tolong** (*help*), **kesian** (*pity*).

In cultivating the national language, Malay is taught in Malaysian school systems, and in the higher learning institutions, with English as the second language. There are various inter-state dialects in the country, such as the dialects of Kelantan, Terengganu, Negeri Sembilan, Kedah, Perak, Johor and so on. The standardized Malay form brings the uniformity of the language system to the official uses in schools, high learning institutions, in the formal governmental administrations and as a communicative language.

Malay is also the national language of Singapore, a nation of 5.5 million directly to the south of Peninsula Malaysia. In addition to the Malay language, Singapore also counts Mandarin, Tamil, and English as official languages. Approximately 13% of Singaporeans use Malay as their mother tongue. It is also the language of their national anthem.

The national language of Indonesia, a country of 250 million inhabitants, is *Indonesian Language,* which the Malay language relates very closely to, has a great number of similarities, and are often mutually intelligible, with both deriving from the *Old Malay*. However, differences in diction, accent, spelling, grammar, pronunciation, and vocabulary require that they be categorized as separate languages. Dutch and Javanese influences are responsible for many of the loanwords variations between the Malay language and Indonesian language.

HOW TO USE THIS BOOK

Learning a language can be compared to a four-legged stool. One has to *speak, listen, read,* and *write*. This guide provides an overview of the grammar. While it is not an exhaustive resource on grammar, it provides basic grammar 'rules'... or rules of thumb. The word 'rules' is in quotation marks, because there are various irregularities. The author has tried to establish and explain these rules, but be aware there may be exceptions (for example, irregular verbs).

Following the grammar section is *essential vocabulary*, arranged by topics such as greetings, food, jobs, etc. There is also a section of non-categorized words at the end of the vocabulary section. There is the list of antonyms for vocabulary development. Learning these antonyms is an excellent way to improve your ability to describe people, places, and conditions. Finally, there is a list of more than 400 common verbs.

One of the simplest ways to use this book is to place a checkmark or dot by each word or phrase that you memorize. If you make it a goal to remember the words you use regularly, you will quickly amass a strong vocabulary. Try to use the grammar rules to express yourself using appropriate conjugations, pluralization and sentence structure. Writing down key phrases and words reinforces memorization. If you are trying to use the book like a dictionary and search for a specific word, first try looking by category from the table of contents. If you do not find it there, look in the list of non-categorized words, or the list of antonyms. If you still cannot find the word, there are some online Malay language dictionaries and apps that will be helpful.

Be aware that as in any language, there are regional differences and multiple ways to say the same thing. The Malay language can be an easy language to learn. You can be speaking basic phrases in a matter of weeks, holding conversations after a few months, and talking almost fluently after a year. Just feel easy to try to communicate. Practice speaking in Malay whenever you can with locals at the markets, the food shops, at landmarks and so on.

Roman Alphabet (Tulisan Rumi)

The **Tulisan Rumi** is the alphabetised Malay writing. Initially, the Malay language was written in Arabic form that is called **Jawi** but the Roman alphabet was officially used in the Malay language after the country's independence in 1957, and further developments in cultivating Malay to the nation as the national language.

Letter	Prounciation	Letter	Prounciation
a	ei	n	en
b	bi	o	ou
c	si	p	pi
d	di	q	kiu
e	i	r	ar
f	ef	s	es
g	ji	t	ti
h	hec	u	yu
i	ai	v	vi
j	je	w	dabelyu
k	kei	x	eks
l	el	y	wai
m	em	z	zed

Pronunciation

Malay Letter	English Example	Malay Example
a	Anna	Nani
b	bar	batik
c	cheek	cara
d	dart	daging
e	pen	penat
f	father	fasih
g	gate	garis
gh	guy	ghairah

h	hazard	hari
i	inner	ini
j	jam	jambatan
k	kart	kata
kh	Loch (Scottish)	khabar
l	Lagos	latar
m	mama	mata
n	noon	naga
ng	darling	jangan
ny	canyon	nyata
o	open	orang
p	papa	padi
q	Qatar	Quran
r	rush	ratus
s	sand	satu
sy	share	syarat
t	tall	tali
u	under	unik
v	vanilla	visa
w	wall	waris
x	X-ray	sinar X
y	yak	kayangan
z	zone	zat

The Diphthongs

Dipthongs are the combination of two vocal sounds uttered in a syllable, by changing the tongue's position.

Malay Diphthongs	English Sound	Malay Example
ai	dye	pakai
au	counter	kalau
oi	oil	amboi

MALAY GRAMMAR

Vocabulary is an extremely important building block of a language. However, grammar is what ties nouns and verbs together to make coherent, descriptive, and meaningful phrases. By combining the basic grammar rules and a broad vocabulary, you can begin to speak the Malay language effectively.

By memorizing the general rules, and adapting to the occasional irregularities, one can manage to learn the language. This section outlines the basic rules of the Malay grammar, including the following:

- Punctuation
- Pronouns
- Demonstrative Adjectives
- Key verbs (to be, to have, to be present)
- Pronouns (subject, object, reflexive)
- Possessive
- Statements
- Questions
- Present tense / Present continuous
-
- Past tense / Past continuous
- Future-tense
- Negatives
- Prepositions
- Imperatives / Obligation / Polite Requests
- Definite articles
- Expressing preference
- Listing things

PUNCTUATION

Following are the names of common punctuation marks. Generally, punctuation is used in the same manner as in English.

English		Malay Equivalent
apostrophe	'	tanda penyingkat
colon	:	kolon
comma	,	koma
exclamation mark	!	tanda seruan
parenthesis	( )	kurungan
period	.	noktah
question mark	?	tanda tanya
quotation marks	"…"	pengikat kata

ASKING QUESTIONS

The Malay language has interrogative words like *who, what, where,* etc. These are among the most important words to memorize.

How much is it?	Berapakah harga ini?
How much?	Berapa harga?
How many?	Berapa?
How?	Bagaimana?
In what way?	Dengan cara apa?
What time is it?	Pukul berapa?
What?	Apa?
What happened?	Apa telah terjadi?
When?	Bilakah?
Where?	Di manakah?
To where?	Ke mana?
Which / Which one?	Yang manakah? / Yang mana satukah?
Who?	Siapa?
For whom?	Untuk siapa?
Whose?	Siapa punya?
Why?	Mengapa?

Within the sentence structure, it is simple to make a *YES / NO* question. One can change the statement into a question just by adding -**kah** to the end of the statement.

Statement:	You like (it).	Kamu suka ini.
Question:	Do you like (it)? (m)	Kamu suka ini**kah**?
Statement:	He has coffee.	Dia minum kopi
Question:	Does he have coffee?	Dia minum kopi**kah**?
Statement:	They are from Penang.	Mereka dari Pulau Pinang.
Question:	Are they from Penang?	Mereka dari Pulau Pinang**kah**?

PERSONAL PRONOUNS

The Malay language requires cultural consideration, politeness to seniority, formality and social status of the person that one interacts with. See the following pronoun table.

Pronouns	Kata Ganti Nama Diri
I	Saya * / Aku
you	awak, kau, engkau, saudara (m), saudari (f)
you (pl/ formal)	kamu*, anda* kalian (plural for you)
he / she	dia
we	kita / kami
they	mereka

*In formal conversations the word **Saya (I), kamu** (*you*) **kalian** (plural for you), and **anda** (*you*) are used.

In English conversations, the pronoun *I* is placed after all the name subjects, e.g. *Anita and I*. In the Malay language, it will be spoken in this way: **Saya dan Anita**. The word **dan** means *and*.

In using *we*, **kita** includes the speaker / listener into the conversing group. For example, *We are Malaysians* is translatated **Kita rakyat Malaysia.** When the listener / reader is excluded, the pronoun expressing *we will be* **(kami)** is used. Observe the following sentences.

*Mum, **we** are going for dinner later.*	Mak, **kami** akan makan malam nanti.
We will be leaving for Kuala Kangsar tomorrow morning.	**Kami** akan bertolak ke Kuala Kangsar pagi esok.

In this context, *mum* was excluded in the group who were going for dinner together. For the second example, the use of **kami** shows the listener is not in the group to travel to Kuala Kangsar.

Kita is used for *we* when the listener is included or when both parties are involved to execute the action.

Let's *clean up this kitchen.*	**Marilah <u>kita</u>** bersihkan dapur ini.
We *are Malaysian citizens.*	**Kita** rakyat Malaysia.

Note that, like English, there is no differentiation in the pronoun between male and female 2nd person (*you*). Also, there is no difference in the pronoun used for *he/she*, the gender of the person being spoken about can be discerned from context.

***I** am from France.*	**Saya** datang dari Perancis.
***She / He** comes from Australia.*	**Dia** dari Australia.
*Where are **you** from?*	**Kamu** dari mana?
***They** are the villagers.*	**Mereka** penduduk kampung ini.

Malaysian society leads a collective way of life. The people always emphasise that they are socially 'related'. Hence, elders are addressed as **pakcik** (*uncle*) and **makcik** (*aunt*). In the use of pronouns, **anda** or **kamu** (*you*) is used in reference to a male or a female. The words **saudara** (*male*) and **saudari** (*saudari*) are the polite way to address a stranger or a person in general. In a casual manner, the pronouns *you* will be used as **awak**, or **engkau** in addressing friends or peers of the same or younger age. **Kalian** is the plural form for *all of you*.

Where are **you** going? (**m**)	**Saudara** hendak ke mana?
Are **you** coming with us? (**f**)	**Saudari** hendak ikut kami?
Kalian boleh pergi bermain.	**All of you** can go to play.
Kamu semua boleh pergi bermain.	**All of you** can go to play.

Demonstrative adjectives

Demonstrative adjectives (*this, that, those, these*) replace nouns. They place emphasis on *specific* things or people. They can also indicate whether they are replacing singular or plural words and give the location of the object. Example: *this* book, *that* cow, *those* people, *these* days; etc

Demonstrative Adjectives	Kata Gantinama Tunjuk
this / these	ini
that / those	itu
here	sini
there	sana, situ

This is my house.	**Ini** rumah saya.
Those are nice.	**Semuanya** cantik.
That is the problem.	**Itu**lah masalahnya.
These are big.	**Semuanya** besar.
Please sit **here.**	Sila duduk **di sini.**
The key is **there.**	Kunci ada **di sana.**

In Malay, *these* and *those* do not have a plural form to them. **Semuanya** is used to mean *all*. However, **semuanya** is not a *demonstrative adjective* under the Malay language grammar.

The use of *either* and *neither* in Malay are as below There is no direct translation for the words individually. Literally translated, *either* means 'one of' and *neither* is 'not one of'.

Either one.	**Salah satu.**
Neither one.	**Tiada satu pun / tiada sesiapa.**
Neither one is going.	Tiada sesiapa yang* pergi.
None are available.	**Tiada** lagi.

* **yang** is a connector in the sentence to show that the rest of the sentence explains the subject in the sentence (**tiada sesiapa**).

REFLEXIVE PRONOUNS

Reflexive pronouns are used to refer the action back to itself. In Malay, there is no single word to each of the reflective pronouns. The word **sendiri** is used typically to represent *self* as a phrase.

Reflexive Pronoun	
myself	saya sendiri / diri saya
yourself (m/f)	kamu sendiri
himself / herself	dia sendiri / dirinya
ourselves	kami sendiri
yourselves (m/f. pl)	kamu sendiri
themselves	mereka sendiri

Examples	
I did it **myself**.	**Saya sendiri** yang melakukannya.
Get it **yourself**.	**Kamu** ambillah **sendiri**.
He hurt **himself**.	**Dia** telah mencederakan **dirinya**.
We love **ourselves**.	**Kami** sayangi **diri kami**.
She loves **herself**.	**Dia** sayangi **dirinya**.

In some context, the pronoun **-nya** is used. It functions as an emphasis term or as a possessive term. If the action is done for oneself, the word **diri**, which means *self*, can be used. The phrase *We love ourselves* would be written as **Kami sayangi diri kami**, and not 'kami sendiri sayang.'

POSSESSIVE

Possessive grammar is used to express ownership of something. One way to show possession is using the possessive pronouns, shown in the following table. The **pronoun** + **punya** by itself shows ownership or possession (mine, yours, etc). In the possessive pronouns for *his*, *hers*, and *its*, that will be changed to use **-nya** to attach to the subject said in the sentence to replace **dia punya**.

Possessive Pronoun	Malay
mine	saya punya
yours	kamu punya
his / hers / its	dia punya
theirs (m/f. pl)	mereka punya
ours	kami punya / kita punya

Examples	Contoh
Is this **his / hers**?	Yang* ini **dia punya**kah?
Is this **yours**?	Yang* ini **kamu punya**kah?
This is **yours**.	Inilah **kamu punya**.
It is **mine**.	Ini **saya punya**./ Inilah saya punya.

*****Yang** as a conjunctive adverb to express the demonstrative adjective

When **-lah** is added to **ini**, it functions to make the sentence less formal, or the sentence becomes friendlier.

In the example sentences above, the word **punya** is used to show possession. However, the possession is not relating to a specifc noun. When the noun in possession is mentioned in the sentence, the word punya is removed, leaving just the pronoun. One very important exeption is the third person (his, her, its) in which instead of the pronoun **dia,** a suffix **-nya** is added to the noun. See example below.

English	Malay	Literal Translation
my job	kerja **saya**	Job I (me)
your job	kerja **kamu** / kerja **anda**	Job you
your job (m/f. pl)	kerja **kalian**	Job you all
his / her job	kerja**nya**	Job his/her
their job	kerja **mereka**	Job they
our job	kerja **kami**	Job we

Notice in these simple sentences below that there is pronoun/possessive, but not a verb. That is because in Malay, the pronoun also implies the verb to be. For example, *Your dog is big* is translated as *Anjing kamu besar*. If literally translated, this would be sound like *Dog you big*.

I love **my wife**.	Saya cinta akan **isteri saya**.
Your dog is big.	**Anjing kamu** besar.
Their car is white.	**Kereta mereka** berwarna putih.
Our baby is a girl.	**Bayi kami** ialah seorang perempuan.
His house is beautiful.	**Rumah<u>nya</u>** cantik.
Her name is Salmah.	**Nama<u>nya</u>** Salmah.
Its horns are sharp.	**Tanduk<u>nya</u>** tajam.
Our country is big.	Negara **kita** besar.
My shoes are white.	**Kasut saya** berwarna putih.
Its price is cheap.	Harga<u>nya</u> murah.

EXPRESSING 'TO BE'

Malay verbs are not conjugated differently for different pronouns, which makes learning the language easier. To express *to be* in the present tense *(I am, she is, they are, etc)* there is no word to substitute *to be* after the pronoun. In the past tense, you just say the *pronoun* + **telah**; (the word **telah** is the past tense indicator. For the present tense negative phrase, **tidak** *(not)* or **bukan** is used after the pronoun. Negative phrases in the past tense are said *exactly* the same way as in the negative present tense phrases. If you are expressing a fact about the past, you must indicate *last week, last time,* etc...

PRESENT		PAST	
I am	Saya	I was	Saya telah
You are	Saudara	You were	Saudara telah
You are (pl)	Kamu	You were (m/f. pl)	Kamu telah
He is / It is	Dia	He was / It was	Dia telah
She is	Dia	She was	Dia telah
They are	Mereka	They were	Mereka telah
We are	Kami	We were	Kami telah
NEGATIVE PRESENT		**NEGATIVE PAST**	
I am not	Saya tidak	I was not	same as neg. present
You are not	Saudara tidak	You were not	same as neg. present
You are not (pl)	Anda / Kamu tidak	You were not (pl)	same as neg. present
He is not	Dia tidak	He was not	same as neg. present
She is not	Dia tidak	She was not	same as neg. present
They are not	Mereka tidak	They were not	same as neg. present
We are not	Kami tidak	We were not	same as neg. present

The word **tidak** is typically used before a verb phrase or an adjective phrase. **Bukan** is used before a noun-phrase or a preposition-phrase.

Negative Present Tense	
We **are not going** to Redang Island.	Kami **tidak pergi** ke Pulau Redang.(verb phrase)
You must not step here.	Kamu **tidak** boleh pijak sini. (verb ph)
Hope it will not rain tonight.	Harap **tidak** akan hujan malam ini.
Lina **is not good** in sewing.	Lina **tidak mahir** dalam jahitan. (adj, phrase)

I **don't** understand this.	Saya **tidak** faham dengan ini.
They **are not lazy.**	Mereka **tidak malas.** (adjective phrase)
The tourist **is not safe**.	Pelancong itu **tidak selamat**. (adj. phrase)
The tourist was not from Ipoh	**Pelancong itu bukan** dari Ipoh. (prep. phrase)
We **are not in** a good situation.	Kami **bukan dalam** keadaan yang baik. (prep. Ph.)
She is not **from Sabah**.	Dia **bukan dari Sabah**. (preposition phrase)
They are not **Janet's relatives.**	Mereka **bukan saudara-mara Janet**. (noun phr.)
He is **not Samad's friend.**	Dia **bukan kawan Samad.** (noun phrase)

The word **ialah** also means *is,* and can be added after the pronoun or noun. It is used to couple the subject to main phrases in the predicate, or used to elaborate on the story in the sentence. It is used before a noun phrase. **Bukan** is word to show the denial element, '*not*', in a noun phrase and the preposition phrase in the sentence.

Examples (Present)

I am a musician from Sabah .	**Saya ialah** ahli muzik **dari** Sabah.
I am not a Chinese.	**Saya bukan** rakyat China.
Sie Ling is a Malaysian.	**Sie Ling ialah** rakyat Malaysia.
You are Samad's friend.	**Anda ialah** kawan Samad.
My friend is an engineer.	**Kawan saya ialah** seorang jurutera.
They are members of this club.	**Mereka ialah** ahli-ahli kelab ini.

Examples (Past)

I was a musician from Kelantan.	**Saya ialah** ahli muzik dari Kelantan.
He was not my manager then.	**Dia bukan** pengurus saya dulu.
Sie Ling was her supervisor.	**Sie Ling ialah** penyelianya.
Rizwan was her supervisor	**Rizwan bukan** penyelianya.
You were the girl I met yesterday.	**Kamu ialah** gadis yang saya nampak.
My friend was an engineer.	**Kawan saya ialah** seorang jurutera.

EXPRESSING 'TO BECOME'

The word **menjadi** means *to become, to be, to happen,* etc. If you want to express something from English such as *I became fat, You became ill,* etc, use **menjadi**, as in examples below.

I **became**...	Saya **menjadi**...		
You **became** ...	Kamu **menjadi**...		
He **became**...	Dia **menjadi** ...		
She **became**...	Dia **menjadi**...		
We **became**...	Kami **menjadi**...		
They **became**...	Mereka **menjadi**...		
She **became** a doctor.	Dia **menjadi** seorang doctor.		

EXPRESSING 'TO HAVE'

The verb *to have* is translated as **ada** or **mempunyai** to express possession. **Ada** and **mempunyai** have the same meanings. When speaking in the past, add the word **pernah** before **ada**. If making the sentence negative, use **tidak** before the verb.

to have – ada / mempunyai

PRESENT		PAST	
I have	Saya ada	I had	Saya pernah ada
You have	Kamu ada	You had	Kamu pernah ada
He has	Dia ada	He had	Dia pernah ada
She has	Dia ada	She had	Dia pernah ada
They have	Mereka ada	They had	Mereka pernah ada
We have	Kami ada	We had	Kami pernah ada

NEGATIVE PRESENT		NEGATIVE PAST	
I don't have	Saya tidak ada	I didn't have	same as neg. present
You don't have (m/f. pl)	Kamu tidak ada	You didn't have	same as neg. present
He does not have	Dia tidak ada	He didn't have	same as neg. present
She does not have	Dia tidak ada	She didn't have	same as neg. present
They do not have	Mereka tidak ada	They didn't have	same as neg. present
We do not have	Kami tidak ada	We didn't have	same as neg. present

Examples

I have a cat.	**Saya ada / mempunyai** seekor kucing.
He does not have a rabbit.	**Dia tidak ada / mempunyai** seekor arnab.
We had clothes.	**Kami ada / mempunyai** pakaian.
You didn't have money.	**Kamu tidak ada / mempunyai** wang.
Malaysia has many natural resources.	**Malaysia ada / mempunyai** banyak sumber semulajadi.
The desert does not have water	**Gurun tidak ada / mempunyai** air.

EXPRESSING 'TO BE PRESENT'

The word **hadir** is used to express that someone or something is present. The word is not conjugated differently; it is the same for all pronouns. When used in the past tense, the word **telah** is added before **hadir.**

to be present - hadir

PRESENT		PAST	
I am **present**	Saya **hadir**	I **was** present	Saya **telah** hadir
You are present	Kamu hadir	You were present	Kamu telah hadir
He is present	Dia hadir	He was present	Dia telah hadir
She is present	Dia hadir	She was present	Dia telah hadir
They are present	Mereka hadir	They were present	Mereka telahhadir
We are present	**Kami** hadir	We **were** present	Kami **telah** hadir

NEGATIVE PRESENT		NEGATIVE PAST	
I am **not** present	Saya **tidak** hadir	I was not present	same as neg. present
You are not present	Kamu tidak hadir	You weren't present	same as neg. present
He / She is not present	Dia tidak hadir	He / She was not present	same as neg. present
They are not present	Mereka tidak hadir	They were not present	same as neg. present
We are not present	Kami tidak hadir	We were not present	same as neg. present

Examples

I am present at the event.	**Saya hadir** di majlis itu.
All of you are present for this activity. (plural)	**Kalian hadir** untuk aktiviti ini.
She was present at the birthday party.	**Dia telah hadir** di majlis ulangtahun itu..
You are not present for the meeting. (singular)	**Kamu tidak hadir** untuk mesyuarat itu.
They are not present yet.	**Mereka** masih **tidak hadir.**
I was not present at the clinic.	**Saya tidak hadir** di klinik itu.
He was present at the clinic.	**Dia telah hadir** di klinik itu.
They were present at the clinic.	**Mereka telah hadir** di klinik itu.
We were not present during the lecture.	**Kami tidak hadir** semasa syarahan itu.

REGULAR VERB PRESENT TENSE

For simple conversation, Malay verbs are exceptionally easy to use since there is no change in the conjugation amongst the pronouns. For example *I go* (**Saya pergi**) features the same verb as *They go* (**Mereka pergi**).

Verb: (to go)	pergi
I **go**…	Saya **pergi**…
You go (m/f)…	Kamu pergi…
You go (pl)…	Kalian pergi…
He goes…	Dia pergi…
She goes…	Dia pergi…
They go …	Mereka pergi…
We go…	Kami pergi…

Verb: (to eat)	makan
I **eat**…	Saya **makan**…
You eat (m/f)…	Kamu makan…
You eat (pl)…	Kalian makan…
He eats…	Dia makan…
She eats…	Dia makan…
We eat…	Kami makan…
They eat (m/f. pl)…	Mereka makan…

Verb: (to speak)	bertutur
I **speak**…	Saya **bertutur**…
You speak (m/f)…	Kamu bertutur…
You speak (pl)…	Kalian bertutur…
He speaks…	Dia bertutur…
She speaks…	Dia bertutur…
We speak…	Kami bertutur…
They speak …	Mereka bertutur …

USING TWO VERBS

The sentence structure of using two verbs in Malay is simple. The pronoun or noun is followed by both verbs, as shown below.

I **want** to **go home**.	Saya **hendak pulang ke rumah**.
He **needs** to **eat**.	Dia **perlu makan**.
Mae **loves** to **work hard**.	Mae **suka** rajin **bekerja**.
They **hate to study**. / They **hate studying**.	Mereka **benci belajar**.
We **like watching** films.	Kami **gemar menonton** filem-filem.
You **like** to **dance**. / You **like dancing**.	Kamu **suka menari**.

GERUNDS

In English, a gerund is the '*ing*' form of a verb, and is often used like a noun. For example, *learning, playing, thinking* are activities. In Malay, the **prefixes 'me-' and 'ber-'** used before verbs turn the verb to gerunds as translated from English. By adding **sedang,** the verbs in malay become present continuous form.

English	Malay
to dance	menari
I am dancing. (present cont)	Saya **sedang menari.**
Dancing is fun.	**Menari** itu menyeronokkan.
to exercise	bersenam
She **is exercising**. (present cont)	Dia **sedang bersenam.**
Exercising everyday is good.	**Bersenam** tiap-tiap hari adalah baik.
to speak	bercakap
She is speaking. (present cont)	Dia **sedang bercakap.**
Speaking a foreign language is hard .	**Bercakap** dalam bahasa asing memang sukar. (**memang** in this context means *is*.)
My favorite activities are **running, singing** and **reading**.	Aktiviti-aktiviti kegemaran saya ialah **berlari, menyanyi** dan **membaca**.

THE PRESENT CONTINUOUS ACTIONS

In the Malay language, when the ongoing actions are spoken, the word **sedang** is used.

She **is bathing**.	Dia **sedang mandi**.
She **is drawing** a picture.	Dia **sedang melukis** gambar.
What are you doing now?	Apakah yang kamu **sedang buat**?
We are fishing by the river.	Kami **sedang memancing** ikan di tepi sungai.

THE PAST TENSE

As shown in the previous verbs, the past tense to a verb in Malay is represented by the word **telah**. It is added to the sentence before the verb (action) to indicate a past action.

Past	Masa Lampau
I **was late** this morning	Saya **terlambat***pagi ini.
You **were early** to work yesterday.	Kamu **telah datang** awal bekerja semalam.
She was awakened by the thunder.	Dia. terjaga* oleh bunyi guruh.
He **wore** a traditional costume to the event.	Dia **telah berpakaian** tradisional ke acara itu.
They **arrived** in Cameron Highlands.	Mereka **telah sampai** ke Cameron Highlands.
We **walked** for three hours just now.	Kami **telah berjalan** kaki / selama tiga jam tadi.

*In another way, the word **telah** can also be replaced by the prefix 'ter-' joined to the verb to indicate the past action.

NEGATIVE STATEMENTS IN THE PRESENT AND PAST TENSES.

In Malay, the word **tidak** (*not*) expresses the negative statements. The phrase **tidak akan** is also used in the statement with actions to show the future situation which will not or had not taken place. The prefix ***'ter-'** and the word **telah** are used before the verbs to represent the past actions in the past tense.

I am not tired.	**Saya tidak** letih.
She does not like **him.**	**Dia tidak** sukakannya.
We do not eat meat.	**Kami tidak** makan daging.
You are not kind.	**Kamu tidak** baik hati.
He is not going out tonight.	**Dia tidak akan** keluar malam ini.
I am not travelling to Java.	**Saya tidak akan** melancong ke Jawa.
They are not going to the waterfalls.	**Mereka tidak akan pergi** ke air terjun.

PAST TENSE NEGATIVE

Negative, past-tense statements in Malay are expressed exactly the same as negative present-tense statements. There is no change. Therefore, if you want it known that the action occurred in the past, you must provide some context (like *last night, yesterday*, etc.) Unlike the past tense positive sentences, the word **telah** is not included.

Past tense positive/negative	Perbuatan masa lampau
I won.	Saya telah menang.
I did not win yesterday.	Saya **tidak** menang semalam.
I read that book.	Saya telah membaca buku itu.
I did not read this book.	Saya **tidak** membaca buku ini.
You played in the rain.	Kamu telah bermain dalam hujan.
You didn't play in the rain.	Dia **tidak** bermain dalam hujan.
You cared.	Kamu telah mengambil berat.
You didn't care.	Anda **tidak** mengambil berat.
She brought the book.	Dia telah membawa buku itu.
She did not bring a book.	Dia **tidak** membawa buku itu.
We remembered.	Kami teringat.
We did not remember.	Kami **tidak** ingat.
They came.	Mereka telah datang.
They did not come.	Mereka **tidak** datang.

Past tense continuous negative and normal past tense are <u>exactly the same</u>. See the following examples.

Past tense	I called.	Saya **telah** menelefon
Past tense negative	I did **not** call.	Saya **tidak** menelefon.
Past continuous	I was calling.	Saya menelefon.
Past continuous neg.	I **was not** calling.	Saya **tidak** menelefon.
Past tense	She bought....	Dia **telah** membeli...
Past tense negative	She did not buy...	Dia **tidak** membeli...
Past continuous	She was buying ...	Dia membeli ...
Past continuous neg.	She **was not** buying...	Dia **tidak** membeli...
Past tense	They sold...	Mereka **telah** menjual...
Past tense negative	They did not sell...	Mereka **tidak** menjual...
Past continuous	They were selling...	Mereka menjual....
Past continuous neg.	They **were not** selling...	Mereka **tidak** menjual...

THE FUTURE TENSE

In the future tense, the word **akan**, which means *will* or *shall,* is added before the verb of a sentence or phrase. **Bolehkah** is translated as *can,* but in this context it means *Will you?*

Future	Akan datang
I **shall be** there early.	Saya *akan berada di sana awal.*
We **shall work** as a team.	Kita **akan bekerja** secara berkumpulan.
She / He **will complete** his course soon.	Dia **akan sempurnakan** kursusnya.
They **will go** to the movies with us.	Mereka **akan pergi** menonton wayang bersama kami.
Kumar **will buy** the ferry ticket tomorrow.	Esok Kumar **akan beli** tiket feri.
Will you help me book a taxi?	**Bolehkah kamu bantu saya** tempah sebuah teksi?
Will they arrive on time?	**Bolehkah mereka sampai** tepat masa?
Will I get on a bus to go to Ipoh?	**Bolehkah saya menaiki** sebuah bas ke Ipoh?
Shall we get some snacks for the picnic?	**Bolehkah kami dapatkan** snek untuk berkelah?

I will eat.	**Saya akan** makan.
He will cook.	**Dia akan** masak.
Sulaiman will visit us.	**Sulaiman akan** melawat kami.
We will wash our hands.	**Kami akan** membasuh tangan.
They will drink.	**Mereka akan** minum.

SENTENCE STRUCTURE BY DIRECT TRANSLATIONS

The Malay sentence structure is made up of a **subject phrase** and a **predicate phrase**, with the subject typically appearing first. The subject can consist of a word or a noun phrase. The predicate is the group of words to explain the story told about the subject. In the below example, *We played in the park yesterday,* the predicate **bermain di taman rekreasi semalam** explained the story of what **Kami** (*we*) did.

ENGLISH SENTENCE	MALAY	THE SUBJECT	THE PREDICATE
She gives him money.	**Dia** memberi wang kepadanya.	Dia	memberi wang kepadanya.
Rama gave money to Litha.	**Rama** telah memberi wang kepada Litha.	Rama	telah memberi wang kepada Litha.
I can come with you.	**Saya** boleh datang bersama kamu	Saya	boleh datang bersama kamu.
We played in the park yesterday.	**Kami** bermain di taman rekreasi semalam.	Kami	bermain di taman rekreasi semalam.
All of them come from Kelantan.	**Mereka semua** datang dari Kelantan.	Mereka semua	datang dari Kelantan.
The group of tourists will set off to Sibu Island.	**Rombongan pelancong itu** akan bertolak ke Pulau Sibu.	Rombongan pelancong itu	akan bertolak ke Pulau Sibu.

OBJECT PRONOUNS

There is not an equivalent of an English object pronoun in Malay. The only difference between the subject pronouns and the object pronouns is in the the use of *him/her* – in which the pronoun '**-nya**' is added to the verb.

Object (English)	Direct Object	Indirect Object
me	saya	saya
you (m/f)	kamu	kamu
you (pl)	kalian	kalian
him	dia	**-nya**
her	dia	**-nya**
them	mereka	mereka
us	kami	kami

Do (it) for **me**.	Lakukannya untuk **saya**.
Do (it) for **us**.	Lakukannya untuk **kami**.
Write (it) for **me**.	Tuliskannya untuk **saya**.
Write (it) for **us**.	Tuliskannya untuk **kami**.

When *it* appears in the sentences, **-nya** must be used to attach to the verb before. E.g. *Pour **it** into my cup* as **Tuangkan<u>nya</u> ke dalam cawan saya.**

I love **you.**	Saya cintakan **kamu.**
I love **her.**	Saya cintakan**nya.**
I love **them.**	Saya cintakan **mereka.**
He loves **her.**	Dia cintakan**nya.**
They love **us.**	Mereka cintakan **kami.**
We love **them.**	Kami cintakan **mereka.**

Do **you** hear **me?**	**Kamu** dengar **saya**kah?
Give **me.**	Berikan kepada **saya.**
Give **him.**	Berikan kepada**nya.**
Give	Berikan

Give the card to **him.**	Berikan kad itu kepada**nya.**
Give the card to **us.**	Berikan kad itu kepada **kami.**

Tell **me.**	Beritahu **saya.**
Tell **them.**	Beritahu **mereka.**
Help **me.**	Tolonglah **saya.**
Help **us.**	Tolonglah **mereka.**

You gave **it** to **me.***	Kamu yang berikan**nya** kepada **saya.**
She gave **that** to **him.***	Dia yang berikan **yang itu** kepada**nya.**
The book is for **you.**	**Buku itu** adalah untuk **kamu.**
It is **for them.**	Yang itu adalah **untuk mereka.**

In the * examples, the **-nya** attached to the verb indicates *it*.

The pronoun *it* does not exist in Malay language. So, the item or subject has to be named in Malay. If it is a human subject, then we can use the pronoun **dia** (*he/she*) E.g.:

I have an extra <u>fork</u>. <u>It</u> is for you. In English, *it* can be used to represent *fork*. However, in the Malay language, the sentences will be translated as **Saya terlebih sebatang <u>garpu (fork)</u>. <u>Garpu (fork)</u> ini adalah untuk kamu.**

about me	mengenai saya / tentang saya.
about you	**mengenai** kamu
about you (pl)	mengenai kalian
about him	mengenainya
about her	mengenainya
about **us**	mengenai **kami**
about them	mengenai mereka
What is it about?	Perkara itu mengenai apa? (Lit: *Issue that about what?*)
The book is about herself.	Buku ini mengenai **dirinya**.
to / for me	kepada / untuk saya
to / for you	kepada / untuk anda
to / for you (pl)	kepada / untuk kamu semua (kalian)
to / for him	kepada / untuknya
to / for her	kepada / untuknya
to / for us	kepada / untuk kami
to / for them	kepada / untuk mereka
*Give it to **them**.*	Berikannya kepada **mereka**.
with me	**dengan** saya
with you	dengan kamu / anda
with **him/her**	denga**nnya**
with **us**	dengan **kami**
with them	dengan mereka
without you	**tanpa** kamu
without him / her	tanpanya
without us	tanpa kami
*Come **without him**.*	Datanglah **tanpanya**.
*I worked **without you**.*	Saya bekerja **tanpa kamu**.
*I sang **with you**. (m)*	Saya menyanyi **dengan kamu**.

IMPERATIVE VERBS

The imperative is a command. In Malay, speaking a command is the same regardless if you are talking to a male, female, or group of people. The only thing that changes is if there is an indirect object (her/him/it, etc) at the end. The word **jangan** is equivalent to *Don't*.

To cancel.	membatalkan
Cancel.	membatalkan
Cancel **it**.	membatalkan**nya**
Don't cancel.	**Jangan** batalkan
Don't cancel **it**.	**Jangan** batalkan**nya**.
To leave	meninggalkan
Leave.	Tinggalkan.
Don't leave.	**Jangan** tinggalkan
Don't leave me.	**Jangan** tinggalkan saya.
Don't leave your things behind.	**Jangan** tinggalkan tinggalkan barang kamu.
To help	menolong.
Help.	menolong.
Help!	Tolong!
Don't help.	**Jangan** tolong.
Don't be late.	**Jangan** lambat.
Don't forget.	Jangan lupa.
Don't come.	Jangan datang.

In the example of *to leave*, the infinitve and imperative are different. *They left their home*, is translated **Mereka tinggalkan rumah mereka**. In this situation, **tinggalkan** or **meninggalkan**, means *to leave* or *vacate* their home.

Tinggalkan is *to* leave when it is used in instructional or command phrases. **Meninggalkan** is *to leave* from a location or a person to show that the action is going on. It also means to vacate from a place or incident.

e.g. :   **Jangan tinggalkanbarang kamu.**
(Don't leave behind your things.)

Mangsa mula meninggalkan kawasan banjir itu.
(The victims started to vacate from the flooded area.)

Why don't you...? in Malay is written as **Mengapakah kamu tidak....?**

Why don't you speak?	**Mengapakah kamu tidak** bercakap?
Why don't you eat?	Mengapakah kamu tidak makan?
Why don't you put on clothes?	Mengapakah kamu tidak berbaju?
Why don't you sleep?	Mengapakah kamu tidak tidur?

SAYING 'WITHOUT'

The words **tanpa** means *without.*

without salt	**tanpa** garam
without sugar	**tanpa** gula

Without money, we cannot live.	**Tanpa** wang, kita tidak boleh hidup.
You cannot not improve **without** practice.	Kamu tidak dapat maju **tanpa** latihan.

EXPRESSING 'ANTI'

The word **anti**, meaning *against*, has the same meaning in both English and Malay.

anti-establishment	anti penubuhan
anti-government	anti kerajaan
anti-biotic	anti biotik

EXPRESSING OBLIGATION

In the Malay language *has to*, *have to* and *need to* can all be represented by the word **perlu** before the verb. The words **mesti** or **mahu,** meaning *must,* can also be used.

I have to go.	Saya **perlu** pergi.
I have to practice.	Saya **perlu** berlatih.
I have to sleep.	Saya **perlu** tidur.
I had to pray.	Saya **perlu** bersembahyang.
I have to work.	Saya **perlu** bekerja.
You have to fight.	Kamu **perlu** melawan.
You have to work.	Kamu **perlu** bekerja.
You had to fight.	Kamu **perlu** melawan.
He has to eat.	Dia **perlu** makan.
He had to try.	Dia **perlu** mencuba.
She has to come.	Dia **perlu** datang.
She has to dance.	Dia **perlu** menari.
They have to vote.	Mereka **perlu** mengundi.
We had to buy food.	Kami **perlu** membeli makanan.

In a different context, the suffix '**–kan**' is added if there is a noun after **perlu**. So **perlukan** is used before a noun or gerund in the sentence.

I **need time** to be examined the samples.	Saya **perlukan masa** untuk periksa sampel-sampel itu.
I **need these books**.	Saya **perlukan buku-buku** ini.
I **need this food** during my journey.	Saya **perlukan makanan ini** dalam perjalanan.
Do you **need this job**?	Anda **perlukan pekerjaan** inikah?
She **needs friends**.	Dia **perlukan kawan-kawan**.
They **need transport** to go to school.	Mereka **perlukan kenderaan** untuk ke sekolah.

POLITE REQUEST

A polite request can be made using the word **bolehkah,** meaning *Is it able* - or – *Is it possible.* The verb for *borrow* is **pinjam**. The verb for *lend* is **pinjamkan**.

Can **you** give me some food?	**Bolehkah kamu** berikan saya sedikit makanan?
Can **you** (plural) work today?	**Bolehkah kamu** semua bekerja hari ini?
Can I watch TV?	**Bolehkah saya** menonton televisyen?

Please, can I **borrow** this?	Bolehkan saya **pinjam** yang ini?
Please **lend** this to me.	Tolong **pinjamkan** ini kepada saya.
Please **lend** me the milk. (imp)	Tolong **pinjamkan** saya susu itu.
Please can I **borrow** some milk?	Bolehkan saya **pinjam** sedikit **susu**?
Please **lend me** a hammer. (imp)	Tolong **pinjamkan saya** sebatang penukul?
Please **can I borrow** a hammer?	**Bolehkah saya pinjam** sebatang penukul?
Please can they **borrow** a hammer?	Bolehkan mereka **pinjam** sebatang penukul?

LET'S / LET US

In English, we use *let us / let's* as a suggestion to do something. It's not as strong as a command or polite as a request, but it is something that is commonly used to direct an action. In Malay, the equivalent terms are **marilah** as *let's* and **biarlah** as *let*. **Biarkan** can also be used under certain contexts, to represent *let*. The suffix **-lah** is used to soften the formality of an action or gives leniency. While **-kan** in a slightly different context shows allowing an action to go on. E.g.: *Let's wait* when translated as **Marilah kita tunggu**, shows the context that *we* (the subject) are voluntarily waiting. **Biarkan kita tunggu** shows that *we want to* wait on until the arrival of what is being waited.

Let us be friends.	**Marilah** kita menjadi kawan.
Let us help each other.	**Marilah** kita saling menolong.
Let's go.	**Marilah** kita pergi.
Let's eat.	**Marilah** kita makan.
Let's wait.	**Marilah** kita tunggu.
Let me sit.	**Biarlah** saya duduk.
Let him sit.	**Biarlah** dia duduk.
Let them eat.	**Biarkan** mereka makan
Let her come.	**Biarkan** dia datang.
Let's get coffee.	**Marilah** kita minum kopi.
Let's see the house.	**Marilah** kita lihat rumah tersebut.
Let me help you.	**Biarlah** saya tolong kamu.
Let me think about it.	**Biarlah** saya fikirkannya.

COMMON PREPOSITION

Following are common Malay prepositions. Examples below show how they are used within a complete sentence.

PREPOSITION	KATA SENDI
about / with regard to	yang di atas / yang mengenai
above	di atas
across	di seberang
after	selepas
ahead of	di hadapan
around (in the area)	keliling
at…o'clock	pada pukul …
at	di
before	sebelum
behind	di belakang
beneath	di bawah
between / among	di antara
beyond	di luar daripada
but	tetapi
by	dengan / di tepi
despite	walaupun
direct / straight	terus
during	semasa
except	kecuali
excluding	tidak termasuk
from	dari / daripada
to	ke / kepada
for	untuk
here it is	di sinilah dia
in the back	di belakang
including	termasuk
in front	hadapan
in front of	di hadapan
like	seperti

near / next to	dekat/ hampir/di sebelah dengan / hampir dengan
not far away	tidak jauh daripada
over / up there	atas
on	di atas
out / outside	luar / di luar
over / up there	atas / di atas
straight on	terus
(turn) to the left	(pusing) ke kiri
(turn) to the right	(pusing) ke kanan
to the side of	ke tepi
under	di bawah
until	sehingga / sampai
with	dengan
without	tiada
within	dalam

They ran **around** the recreational park.	Mereka berlari **mengelilingi** taman rekreasi itu.
We are travelling **to Penang.**	Kami melancong **ke Pulau Pinang.**
The document was sent to Mr. Chung.	Dokumen itu telah **dihantar kepada** Encik Chung.
Where is the tourist **from**?	Pelancong itu datang **dari mana**? (The tourist/ comes/ from where?)
This pot is **made from** ceramic.	Pasu itu **dibuat daripada** seramik.
… **from** Dublin **to** Bangkok.	… **dari** Dublin **ke** Bangkok.
That accident was **beyond** our control.	Kemalangan itu **di luar daripada** kawalan kami.

We go **after** class.	Kami pergi **selepas** kelas.
It is **like** a cat.	Ini **seperti** seekor kucing.
It is **near** my house.	Itu **berdekatan dengan** rumah saya.
That is **on the table**.	Yang itu **di atas** meja.
It is **across** the street.	Itu ada **di seberang** jalan.
It is **behind** the house.	Itu ada di belakang rumah.

From here / From there.	Dari sini / Dari sana.
To there	Ke sana
something / nothing	sesuatu / tiada apa
anything / everything	apa-apapun / semuanya
Everything, **except** milk.	Semuanya, **kecuali** susu.
Between Georgetown **and** Ipoh.	**Di antara** Georgetown **dan** Ipoh
Not far **from** Melaka.	Tidak jauh **dari** Melaka

PREPOSITION PHRASING

As in English, prepositions are used in Malay to describe locations or situations. Following are examples that further help to understand the order in which prepositions are situated in Malay sentences. Prepositions in English and Malay are in bold text.

She went **to the** office.	Dia telah pergi **ke** pejabat.
Literally: *She went to the office.*	
He came **from his** farm.	Dia datang **dari** ladangnya.
Literally: *He came from farm his.*	
Turn **to the** left, **after** the river.	Belok ke kiri, selepas sungai itu.
Literally: *Turn to left, after river the.*	
We are **among** the Malay people.	Kamilah **antara** orang Melayu.
Literally: *We are among the people Malay.*	
The food is **on** the table	Makanan ada **di atas** meja.
Literally: *Food have on table.*	
During the war, we are **without** peace.	Ketika peperangan, kita **tiada** ketenangan.
Literally: *During war, we **don't have** peace.*	

PLURALIZING NOUNS

When a noun is pluralized, it indicates more than one of a particular object. For instance, *mouse* becomes *mice* or *plane* becomes *planes*. The Malay language uses a double word to express plural nouns. See examples below.

English (singular)	Malay (singular)	English (pl)	Malay (plural)
bed	katil	beds	katil-katil
book	buku	books	buku-buku
car	kereta	cars	kereta-kereta
cat	kucing	cats	kucing-kucing
country	negara	countries	negara-negara
hand	tangan	hands	tangan-tangan
hill	bukit	hills	bukit-bukau**
house	rumah	houses	rumah-rumah
mountain	gunung	mountains	gunung-ganang**
paper	kertas	papers	kertas-kertas
person	orang	people	manusia*
place	tempat	places	tempat-tempat
problem	masalah	problems	masalah-masalah
tooth	gigi	teeth	gigi-gigi

There are exceptions to the pluralization by duplication of Malay nouns. For example, the following:

* The plural form of **orang** cannot be a double word, but instead uses **manusia**. The word **orang-orang** in Malay means the *scarecrow*.

** The double words for *hills* is not **bukit-bukit** but written as the rhythmic **bukit-bukau** and mountain is not **gunung-gunung**, but as **gunung-ganang**.

EXPRESSING 'THE' (DEFINITE ARTICLE)

In English, *the* is used to specify something specific. To indicate this definite article, the word **tersebut** is used after the specific noun. It means *The said...* in the Malay language.

GENERAL	girl	gadis
SPECIFIC	**the** girl	gadis **tersebut**
GENERAL	job	pekerjaan
SPECIFIC	**the** job	pekerjaan **tersebut**
GENERAL	mountain	gunung
SPECIFIC	**the** mountain	gunung **tersebut**
GENERAL	food	makanan
SPECIFIC	**the** food	makanan **tersebut**
GENERAL	**country**	negara
SPECIFIC	**the country**	negara **tersebut**
GENERAL	class	kelas
SPECIFIC	**the** class	kelas **tersebut**

That is a girl.	Itu seorang perempuan (gadis).
The girl is smart.	Gadis **tersebut** pandai.
You need a job.	Kamu perlukan pekerjaan.
The job has a good salary.	Pekerjaan **tersebut** bergaji lumayan.
There are **mountains**.	Di sana ada gunung-ganang
I want to climb **the** mountain	Saya hendak mendaki gunung **tersebut**.
I like food.	Saya suka makanan.
I like **the** food at this restaurant.	Saya suka makanan **tersebut** di restoran ini.
I don't like going to class.	Saya tidak suka mengikuti pelajaran.
The class is boring.	Pelajaran **tersebut** sungguh membosankan.

Tersebut when literally translated means *as said*. So, **tersebut** becomes the definite article *the.* in the sentences above.

EXPRESSING 'WHEN' or 'WHILE'

The following table shows examples of how to express particular moments in time. In English, we say *when* or *while* to express a moment in the present, past, or future. For example, *when I was young*, *when I get rich*, etc. In Malay, this is most simply expressed with the word **apabila** followed by the remainder of the sentence. See the following table and example phrases.

When I …	**Apabila** saya…
When you (m/f) …	**Apabila** kamu…
When you (pl)…	**Apabila** kalian …
	Apabila kamu semua…
When he (it) …	**Apabila** dia …
When she …	**Apabila** dia …
When they …	**Apabila** mereka …
When we …	**Apabila** kami…

When we have money…	**Apabila kami** ada duit (wang*)….
When you have children…	**Apabila kamu** ada anak ….
When they come…	**Apabila mereka** datang ….

*Some people will use **wang** instead of **duit** in their speeches to mean *money*. **Duit** and **wang** have the same meaning.

If the phrase is to express something in the past, the phrase **Ketika itu** can be used.

During that time…	**Ketika itu** …
During that time, grandmother was ill.	**Ketika itu**, nenek telah sakit.
When I was in school….	**Ketika** saya di sekolah …
When she was ill…	**Ketika** dia sakit …
When you were young…	**Ketika** kamu muda …
When they were working…	**Ketika** mereka bekerja ….

The word **lebih suka** is used to express something is preferable or better than something else.

I prefer …	Saya **lebih suka** ...
You prefer (m/f)…	Kamu **lebih suka** …
You prefer (pl)…	Kamu semua **lebih suka** …
He prefers ….	Dia **lebih suka** …
She prefers …	Dia **lebih suka** …
They prefer …	Mereka **lebih suka** …
We prefer …	Kami **lebih suka** …

Do you **prefer** tea or coffee?	Kamu **lebih suka** teh atau kopi?
Which do you **prefer**?	Kamu **lebih suka** yang mana satu?
He prefers to drink coffee.	Dia **lebih suka** minum kopi.
You prefer to eat rice.	Kamu **lebih suka** makan nasi.
I like wine more **compared to** beer.	Saya lebih suka wain **berbanding** bir.

COMPARING THINGS

In English when something is compared, we often add -*er* to the adjective; for example, *shorter than, happier than, bigger than*, etc. In English, we might say *shorter* or *shortest*. The equivalent in Malay will be like:

She is **more** intelligent.	Dia **lebih** cerdik.
At football, he is **worse than** Billy.	Dalam permainan bola sepak, dia **lebih teruk daripada** Billy.

To express something is *as good as*, use **sebaik.** The affix 'se-….' is added before the adjective to show as ... as or both matters have the similar qualities.

Betty is **as good as** Jean in grilling fish.	Betty adalah **sebaik** Jean dalam membakar ikan.
Cycling is **as healthy** as swimming.	Berbasikal adalah **sesihat** berenang.
This buiding **is as tall** as that building.	Bangunan ini adalah **setinggi dengan** bangunan itu.

The word **seperti** is also used to express *like* or *similar*. Both words are used between the nouns they are comparing:

The Malaysian weather **is like** Cuba.	Cuaca di Malaysia adalah **seperti** di Cuba.
Kuala Lumpur **is like** Bangkok.	Kuala Lumpur adalah **seperti** Bangkok.

When the comparison of adjective is used between two items, **lebih ... daripada** will be used to show *more than*.

Wine is **more expensive than** beer.	Wain **lebih mahal daripada** bir.
Perak is **bigger than** Malacca.	Perak **lebih besar daripada** Melaka.
Melisa is **younger than** Dylan.	Melisa lebih muda daripada Dylan.
We **are better** in playing badminton **than** in Frisbee.	Kami **lebih baik** dalam badminton **daripada** Frisbee.

In the superlative forms, the is represented by the affix **ter-** before the adjective, to show the that functions to show the superlative form of an adjective.

She is **the prettiest** of all the girls.	Dialah yang **tercantik** antara semua gadis.
Your embroidery is **the best**.	Sulaman andalah yang **terbaik.**
Eric is **the tallest** man in the team.	Eric adalah **yang tertinggi** dalam pasukan itu.
He is **the richest** man in the city.	Dialah lelaki **yang terkaya** di bandaraya ini.
Janet is the **smartest**.	Janet adalah yang **terpandai.**
The Scandinavia is **the most advanced** region.	Negara Skandinavia merupakan kawasan **yang termaju**.

There are at least four ways to say *VERY*. They are **sungguh, sangat, amat benar, and amat betul.** These can basically be used interchangeably.

SAYING ABOUT

In a previous section on prepositions, it is shown that *about me / about you* etc is expressed using the word **mengenai** (*relating to*). To express approximation of something (like a value), use the phrase **lebih kurang** which means **more or less** (approximately).

What is the film **about**?	Filem itu **mengenai** apa?
The film is **about** monkeys.	Filem itu **mengenai** monyet-monyet.
Who are you talking **about**?	Kamu bercakap **mengenai** siapa?
What is that story **about**?	Cerita itu **mengenai** apa?
It's **about** $100.	Itu **lebih kurang** seratus dolar.
They will arrive **about** ten o'clock.	Mereka akan tiba **lebih kurang** pukul sepuluh.

TO MISS SOMETHING

In English, the verb *to miss* is used in several different ways. Use the following examples to understand how to translate the different meanings of *miss* in Malay conversation.

- If you are missing a person, use the verb **rindu akan**
- If you missed a bus, plane, or appointment, use the verb the word **tertinggal**
- If you are missing a material item, use the word **telah hilang**

I **miss** my mother.	Saya **rindu akan** ibu saya.
I **miss** my husband.	Saya **rindu akan** suami saya.
I **missed** the bus.	Saya **tertinggal** bas.
She misses her breakfast.	Dia **tertinggal** sarapan paginya.
I am **missing** (searching for) my shoe.	Kasut saya **telah hilang.** (Lit: Shoes my lost.)
My dog **is missing (lost).**	Anjing saya **telah hilang**. (Lit: Dog my lost.)

AND / OR

The conjunction *and* in English to join nouns is expressed as **dan** in Malay.

mother **and** child	ibu **dan** anak
bread **and** tea	roti **dan** teh
cars **and** horses	kereta **dan** kuda
I want eggs, milk, and bread.	Saya mahu telur, susu **dan** roti.

The word **atau** is the Malay equivalent the word '*or*' and are used similar to English to separate two or more things.

This or that?	Yang ini **atau** yang itu?
Black or white?	Hitam **atau** putih?
Tea or coffee?	The **atau** kopi?
I will take **chicken** or **beef**.	Saya akan ambil **ayam** atau **daging lembu**.

MALAY AFFIXES

Many resources on the Malay language tend to focus on the various affixes (prefixes and suffixes) that are merged on to the root words, thus creating a plethora of new words and derivations. The authors of this book feel that while understanding the use of affixes can be useful to your understanding of the Malay language, their complexity makes it not recommended to spend a large amount of time studying, when one could simply memorize the word needed (rather than derive it through some type of rule or formula.) This guide is for beginnners and intermediate speakers of Malay. Using the affixes fluently is something that can be be picked up gradually through practice and interactions in utterance. Several expamples follow. As you can observe, the use of the affixes is somewhat complex, and not easily explained by grammar rules. Thus, word by word memorization is encouraged.

Affix	Word: laku	Example	Translation
meN-....kan	melakukan	Kami suka **melakukan** kerja amal.	We like **to do** charity work.
beR-	berlaku	Gempa bumi **telah berlaku**.	An earthquake **happened.**
di-...kan	dilakukan	Cubaan baik **telah dilakukan** oleh mereka.	A good trial **has been done** by them.
ke...an	kelakuan	**Kelakuan** Dina baik.	Dina's **behaviour** is good.

THE HIBISCUS FLOWER.

GREETINGS	UCAPAN
Welcome.	Selamat datang
Hello / Hi.	Salam, Hai
How are you?	Apa khabar?
How is your family? `	Apa khabar keluarga anda?
They are fine.	Mereka baik.
They are not good.	Mereka kurang baik.
How's life?	Apa khabar?
How's it going? (informal)	Kamu macam mana?
Are you alright?	Kamu baikkah? / Kamu sihatkah?
I am alright.	Saya tidak apa-apa.
Fine / I am fine.	Khabar baik / Baik-baik belaka
Fine / I am fine.	Khabar baik / Baik-baik belaka
Very well.	Baik-baik belaka / Sihat-sihat belaka
Praise be to God	Segala puji-pujian bagi Tuhan
Good morning.	Selamat pagi.
Good afternoon.	Selamat tengahari.
Good day	Selamat sejahtera
Good evening.	Selamat petang.
Good night.	Selamat malam.
How was your night?	Bagaimanakah kamu malam tadi?
How was your day?	Bagaimanakah kamu hari ini?
How was your evening?	Bagaimanakah kamu petang tadi?
Good bye.	Selamat jalan / Selamat tinggal.
Have a good day.	Selamat sejahtera
See you later.	Jumpa lagi / Jumpa nanti.
I am happy to meet you.	Saya berasa gembira berkenalan dengan kamu.
May God give you health.	Semoga tuhan memberkati kesihatan
My name is _____.	Nama saya _____.
My name is _____.	Saya bernama_____.

*What is your **name**?*	Siapa nama kamu?
*What's her **name**?*	Siapa namanya?
name	nama
Pardon me (Excuse me).	Maafkan saya.
Pardon me, I forgot your name.	Maafkan saya, saya terlupa nama kamu.

MAKING CONVERSATION	**PERTUTURAN**
Where are you from?	Kamu dari mana?
What are you doing here?	Kamu buat apa di sini?
Are you adjusting here?	Kamu boleh menyesuaikan diri di sini?
I'm adapting to it.	Saya masih menyesuaikan diri.
How old are you?	Berapakah umur kamu?
How long have you been here?	Berapa lamakah kamu telah berada di sini?
Where have you been?	Ke manakah kamu telah pergi?
I am here.	Saya ada di sini.

BASIC PHRASES	**FRASA ASAS**
Yes / No	Ya / Tidak
Can you?	Kamu boleh?
Congratulations!	Tahniah!
*Can you speak **English**?*	Bolehkah kamu bertutur dalam **Bahasa Inggeris**?
good / bad	baik / tidak baik / buruk
Help!	Tolong!
How do I find___?	Bagaimanakah saya cari ____?
How do you say___?	Bagaimanakah kamu kata ____?
However,	Walau bagaimanapun,
I am ___	Saya____
I am slowly learning	Saya masih belajar perlahan-lahan.
I am not___.	Saya tidak / bukan____.
I can.	Saya boleh.
I cannot.	Saya tidak boleh.

I don't care.	Saya tidak peduli.
I have___.	Saya ada ____.
I don't have.	Saya tidak ada ____.
I want___.	Saya mahu ____.
I don't want ____.	Saya tidak mahu _____.
I like ____ very much.	Saya suka sangat _____.
I like / love____.	Saya suka ____.
I don't like / love.	Saya tidak suka ____.
I speak____	Saya bertutur _____.
I don't speak____.	Saya tidak boleh bertutur ____.
I prefer ____.	Saya lebih suka ___.
It doesn't matter.	Itu tidak penting
It is ____.	Itu ialah____.
It is not ____.	Itu bukan ____.
It's very good.	Itu sangat baik.
like that	macam itu
like this	macam ini
No!	Tidak!
Okay	Boleh / Ya.
Please	Tolong / Silakan
Speak slowly.	Cakap perlahan sedikit.
Sure.	Ya.
Thank you.	Terima kasih.
Thanks to God.	Terima kasih Tuhan
You're welcome. (response to thank you)	Sama-sama.
There is ____.	Itu ialah ____.
There is not / none.	Itu bukan ____.
What are you doing?	Apakah yang sedang kamu buat?

MORE BASICS	ASAS
Are you ready?	Kamu sudah bersediakah?
Are you sure?	Adakah kamu /anda pasti?

By the way,	Dengan cara itu,
Can I help you?	Bolehkah saya tolong kamu?
Excuse me. (Pardon me)	Minta maaf / maaf saya
I agree with you.	Saya bersetuju dengan anda.
I am busy. / I don't have time.	Saya sedang sibuk / Saya tiada masa.
I am drinking.	Saya sedang minum.
I believe ____	Saya percaya ___.
I gave you.	Saya yang berikan kamu.
I know her / him.	Saya kenal dia.
I promise.	Saya berjanji.
I can see it	Saya boleh nampaknya.
I will help you	Saya akan tolong kamu.
I will wait for you.	Saya akan tunggu kamu.
I'm bringing____.	Saya akan membawa ____.
I'm waiting.	Saya sedang menunggu.
if…	kalau / sekiranya
if not…	kalau tidak / sekiranya tidak
if so	kalau begitu
It's not a problem.	Itu bukannya masalah.
instead of…	dan bukannya
*May we order fried rice **instead of** noodles?*	Bolehkah kami pesan nasi goreng **dan bukannya** mi?
Introduce myself.	Memperkenalkan diri saya.
Is it possible?	Mungkinkah ini?
It is not possible.	Ini tidak mungkin.
It is possible.	Ini mungkin.
It seems to me that…	Ini kelihatan bahawa___
Let me think about it.	Biar saya fikirkannya dahulu.
Me too.	Saya juga.
My favorite	Kesukaan saya / kegemaran saya
my opinion	pandangan saya
In my opinion	Pada pandangan saya

Not now.	Bukan sekarang.
One moment.	Sekejap.
Sorry, I'm late.	Maaf, saya terlambat.
Thank you for helping me.	Terima kasih kerana menolong saya.
Thank you for coming.	Terima kasih kerana sudi datang.
Thank you for everything.	Terima kasih untuk semua.
Thank you.	Terima kasih.
Wait for me.	Tunggu saya.
Let us share.	Marilah kita berkongsi.
Will you bring _____?	Kamu akan membawa _____?
*Will you help **me**?*	Kamu akan membantu **saya**?
Is that suitable?	Adakah itu sesuai?
That works for me.	Yang itu boleh untuk saya.
That doesn't work for me.	Yang itu tidak boleh untuk saya.
What do you think (about)...?	Apakah pandangan kamu (tentang)...?
What do you think?	Apakah pandangan kamu?

EXPRESSING CONFUSION	**MENERANGKAN KEKELIRUAN**
I am confused.	Saya keliru.
Are you confused?	Kamu kelirukah?
Do you remember?	Kamu ingatkah?
Do you understand?	Kamu fahamkah?
Yes, I understand.	Ya, saya faham.
I didn't forget.	Saya tidak lupa.
I don't know.	Saya tidak tahu.
I don't understand.	Saya tidak faham.
I forgot.	Saya terlupa.
I remember now.	Saya ingat sekarang.
I'm not sure	Saya kurang pasti.
I'm thinking	Saya sedang berfikir.
misunderstanding	Salahfaham.
Please repeat .	Tolong ulang lagi.
What did you say just now?	Apa kamu katakana tadi?

What does it mean?	Apa maksudnya ini?
What is it?	Apa itu?

COLOURS	WARNA
black	hitam
blue	biru
blue (light)	biru muda
blue (dark)	biru tua
brown	perang (pronounce: pay-rung) / coklat
gray	kelabu
green	hijau
gold	emas
orange	jingga / oren
pink	merah jambu
purple	ungu
rainbow colours	warna pelangi
red	merah
red (light)	merah muda
red (dark)	merah tua
silver	perak
white	putih
yellow	kuning
green *hill.*	bukit **hijau**.
My favourite colour is blue.	Warna kegemaran saya ialah **biru**.

EMOTIONS	EMOSI
How are you?	Apa khabar?
affection	sayang
anger	marah
anxious	gelisah
boredom	bosan
cry	menangis
despair	putus asa
emotions / feelings	emosi
fear	takut

fearless	tidak takut
feeling	rasa
frightening	takut
fun	seronok
funny	kelakar / lucu
happiness / joy	kegembiraan
hope	harapan
hopeful	ada harapan/ berharapan
hopeless	tiada harapan
laugh	gelak / ketawa
loneliness	sepi
love	cinta
panic	cemas
sad	sedih
smile	senyum
stress	tertekan
stressful	tekanan
tiresome	meletihkan
unhappy	tidak gembira / sedih
worry	risau / bimbang
Are you crying?	Kamu menangis?
Don't cry.	Jangan menangis.
Don't worry	Jangan risau.
I am angry.	Saya berasa marah.
I am happy	Saya berasa gembira.
I am sad.	Saya berasa letih.
That is funny.	Ini lucunya.
That is interesting.	Itu menarik.
That is fun.	Itu menyeronokkan

NOISE AND MUSIC	**BUNYI DAN MUZIK**
disturbance/bother	gangguan
drum	dram
guitar	gitar
loud	bising

melodious	merdu
music	muzik
musical instrument	alat muzik
noise	bunyi
noisy	bising
party	jamuan
rough voice, hoarse	serak
scream / shout	jeritan
silence / quiet	kesunyian / sunyi
song	lagu
sound	bunyi
stereo	stereo
voice	suara
Increase the volume.	Tinggikan suara.
Lower the volume.	Rendahkan suara.

LIGHTING AND COLOURS	PENCAHAYAAN DAN WARNA
black	hitam
bright (very)	(sangat) terang
candle light	cahaya lilin
dark colour	warna tua
dim	malap
fluorescence	pendarfluor
fluorescent bulbs	mentol pendarfluor
glare	bersilau
gray	kelabu
hue	warna
illumination	pencahayaan
light	cahaya
light colour	warna muda
rainbow colours	warna pelangi
ray	sinaran
tone	ton warna
white	putih

NUMBERS	NOMBOR
0 – zero	sifar / kosong
1 – one	satu
2 – two	dua
3 – three	tiga
4 – four	empat
5 – five	lima
6 – six	enam
7 – seven	tujuh
8 – eight	lapan
9 – nine	sembilan
10 – ten	sepuluh
11 – eleven	sebelas
12 – twelve	dua belas
13 – thirteen	tiga belas
14 – fourteen	empat belas
15 – fifteen	lima belas
16 – sixteen	enam belas
17 – seventeen	tujuh belas
18 – eighteen	lapan belas
19 – nineteen	sembilan belas
20 – twenty	dua puluh
21 – twenty one	dua puluh satu
25 – twenty five	dua puluh lima
30 – thirty	tiga puluh
32 – thirty two	tiga puluh dua
34- thirty four	tiga puluh empat
36-thirty six	tiga puluh enam
40 – forty	empat puluh
50 – fifty	lima puluh
60 – sixty	enam puluh

70 – seventy	tujuh puluh
80 – eighty	lapan puluh
90 – ninety	sembilan puluh
100 – one hundred	seratus
156	seratus lima puluh enam
thousand	seribu
1500	seribu lima ratus
1050	seribu lima puluh
million	sejuta
€15	**lima belas** Euro
£26	**dua puluh** enam Pound Sterling
¥50 000	**lima puluh** ribu Yen
⅔	dua per tiga
⅞	tujuh per lapan
0.2	kosong perpuluhan dua /kosong poin dua
44.35	empat puluh empat poin tiga lima
25**%** discount	dua puluh lima **peratus** diskaun
6**%** GST	enam **peratus** GST
10 % service charges	sepuluh peratus caj perkhidmatan
15% reimbursement	lima belas peratus bayaran balik

CARDINAL NUMBERS	BILANGAN TEMPAT
first	pertama
second	kedua
third	ketiga
fourth	keempat
fifth	kelima
last	akhir

QUANTITIES	BILANGAN
both	kedua-dua
single	satu
double	dua / sepasang
multiple	beberapa
one half	setengah / separuh

one third	se pertiga
one fourth	suku
one tenth	se per sepuluh
one whole	kesemua

TIME EXPRESSION	MENYATA MASA
What time is it?	Pukul berapa?
It is 10:00.	Pukul sepuluh.
It is a quarter after 10:00.	Pukul sepuluh suku.
It is 10:30.(half past ten)	Pukul sepuluh setengah.
It is 10:45.	Pukul sepuluh empat puluh lima.
It is a quarter to 2:00.(1:45)	Pukul satu empat puluh lima.
At _____ o'clock.	Pada pukul _____.
almost	dekat
already	sudah
finally	akhirnya
not yet	belum
previously	sebelum itu
recently	baru-baru ini
now	sekarang

TIME OF THE DAY	WAKTU
daybreak	siang
morning	pagi
noon	tengahari
afternoon	petang (12:01-sunset)
evening	petang
night	malam
midnight	tengah malam

TIME UNITS	UNIT MASA
second	saat
minute	minit
half hour	setengah jam

hour	satu jam
day	hari
daily	harian
every day	tiap-tiap hari
week	minggu
weekly	mingguan
month	bulan
monthly	bulanan
year	tahun
annual / yearly	tahunan
decade	dekad
era / generation	era / zaman /generasi
century	abad

ABOUT THE TIME	MENGENAI MASA
*What is **the date**?*	Apakah **tarikh**nya?
What is the day today?	Hari ini hari apa?
Today is Tuesday, 6 October.	Hari ini hari Selasa, 6 Oktober.
after	selepas
before	sebelum
date	haribulan
day after tomorrow	lusa
day before yesterday	hari sebelum semalam
day to day	hari ke hari
during	semasa
early	awal
every	setiap / tiap-tiap
future	akan datang
last	akhir
last time	dahulu
last year	tahun lepas
late	lewat
late last year	lewat tahun lepas
later	kemudian
latest / most recent	terkini

next	seterusnya
Now a days	kini
past	selepas
period / time / duration	masa/ jangka masa
present time / currently	sekarang / kini
previous	sebelum itu
soon	tidak lama lagi
then	kemudian
today	hari ini
tomorrow	esok
tonight	malam ini
up coming	akan datang
yesterday	semalam

FREQUENCY	KEKERAPAN
always	selalu
every time	setiap kali
never	belum
often	selalu / sentiasa
seldom / rarely	bukan selalu
sometimes	kadang-kadang
time after time	dari masa ke masa
usually	biasanya

MONTHS	BULAN
January	Januari
February	Februari
March	Mac
April	April
May	Mei
June	Jun
July	Julai
August	Ogos
September	September

October	Oktober
November	November
December	Disember

The legendary moon fairy, Chang Er by C. Mouyon

DAYS OF THE WEEK	HARI
Sunday	Ahad
Monday	Isnin
Tuesday	Selasa
Wednesday	Rabu
Thursday	Khamis
Friday	Jumaat
Saturday	Sabtu
weekend	hujung minggu

FAMILY	KELUARGA
husband	suami
wife	isteri
father	bapa / ayah
mother	emak / ibu
son	anak lelaki

daughter	anak perempuan
brother (older)	abang
brother (younger)	adik lelaki
sister (older)	kakak
sister (younger)	adik perempuan
uncle	bapa saudara
aunt	emak saudara
cousin	sepupu
mother-in-law	ibu mertua
father-in-law	bapa mertua
son-in -law	menantu
daughter-in-law	menantu
step son	anak lelaki tiri
step daughter	anak perempuan tiri
grandfather	datuk
grandmother	nenek
grandchildren	cucu
baby	bayi
children	kanak-kanak
family	keluarga
parent / parents	ibubapa
relative	saudara

GENDER	JANTINA
best friend	kawan karib
boy	lelaki
boyfriend	teman lelaki
female	perempuan
friend	kawan / rakan / sahabat
friendship	persahabatan
girl	perempuan
girlfriend	teman wanita
male	lelaki

man	jejaka / lelaki
Mr.	Encik / En.
Mrs.	Puan / Pn.
Ms.	Cik
neighbour	jiran
woman	wanita

ROMANCE / LOVE	CINTA
Do you love me?	Kamu mencintai saya?
I love you.	Saya cintakan kamu.
I am in love.	Saya dilamun cinta.
I admire you.	Saya mengkagumi anda / kamu.
Are you married?	Kamu sudah berkahwin?
I am divorced.	Saya sudah bercerai.
I am married.	Saya sudah berkahwin.
I am not married.	Saya belum berkahwin.
I am going to marry soon.	Saya akan kahwin tidak lama lagi.
I am single.	Saya masih bujang.
I miss you.	Saya rindu kamu.
You are beautiful.	Kamu cantik.
You are handsome.	Kamu segak.

SEXUALITY	KESEKSUALAN
birth control	kawalan kelahiran
condom	kondom

homosexual	homoseksual
menstruation	haid
pregnant / pregnancy	hamil / mengandung
lover / sweetheart	kekasih
sexual intercourse	hubungan seks

ORGANS	ORGAN DALAMAN
bladder	pundi kencing
brain	otak
heart	jantung
intestine	usus
kidney	ginjal / buah pinggang
liver	hati
lung	paru-paru
stomach	perut
uterus	rahim

THE HEAD	BAHAGIAN KEPALA
beard	janggut
cheek	pipi
chin	dagu
ear	telinga
eye	mata
eyebrow	kening mata
eyelash	bulu mata
forehead	dahi
head	kepala
hair	rambut
jaw	rahang
lip	bibir
moustache	misai
mouth	mulut
nose	hidung

teeth / tooth	gigi
throat	tekak
tongue	lidah

BODILY FLUID	**BENDALIR BADAN**
blood	darah
breast milk	susu ibu
mucus	mukus
poop / feaces	najis
pee / urine	kencing
pus	nanah
saliva / spit	air liur
sperm / semen	sperma / air mani
sweat	peluh
tears	air mata
vaginal fluid	cecair faraj
vomit	muntah

MEDICAL TERMINOLOGY	**ISTILAH / TERMINOLOGI PERUBATAN**
abortion	keguguran
AIDS	AIDS
allergic	alahan
anesthesia	bius
antibiotic	antibiotik
antiseptic	antiseptik
bandage	pembalut
bleeding	pendarahan
cancer	kanser / barah
chill	kesejukan
cleft lip	bibir rekah
contagious	berjangkit
constipation	sembelit
cough / cold	batuk /selsema

cure / medicine	sembuh / ubat
dehydration	dehidrasi
diagnosis	diagnosis
diarrhea	cirit-birit
digestion	penghadaman
disease	penyakit
dizziness	pening
doctor	doktor
fever	demam
food poisoning	keracunan makanan
gastritis	gastritis
goiter	beguk
head ache	Sakit kepala
HIV	HIV
hunger	lapar
immunisation	immunisasi
infection	jangkitan / infeksi
itchy	gatal
lice	kutu
malaria	malaria
massage	urut
medication	ubat-ubatan
migraine	migrain
nausea	loya
pain	kesakitan, sakit
patient	pesakit
pharmacy	farmasi
poisonous/toxic	beracun
pregnancy	kehamilan
rabies (mad dog sickness)	penyakit anjing gila
sexually transmited disease	penyakit
sick / ill	sakit
sore	sakit

sprain	terseliuh
stomach ache	sakit perut
surgery	pembedahan
swelling	bengkak
tape warm	cacing pita
tuberculosis	batuk kering
to vomit	muntah
tooth ache	sakit gigi
tuberculosis (tb)	batuk kering / penyakit T.B
typhoid	demam kepialu
vaccination	vaksin

BODILY FUNCTION	**FUNGSI BADAN**
belch / burp	sendawa
breath	pernafasan
fart	buang angin
give birth	melahirkan
sleep	tidur
snore	berdengkur
whistle	bersiul
sneeze	bersin
yawn	menguap

DISABILITY	**KECACATAN**
blind	buta
crippled	lumpuh
deaf	pekak
deformity	kecacatan
dementia	demensia
disability	kurang upaya / kecacatan
disabled	orang kurang upaya
dwarf	kerdil
injured	tercedera
insane	tidak waras

limp	tempang
paralyzed	lumpuh
wheel chair	kerusi roda

HEALTH RELATED CONVERSATIONS	PERBUALAN MENGENAI KESIHATAN
Are you better?	Kamu rasa lebih baik?
I feel better.	Saya berasa baik. / Saya berasa sihat
Are you sick?	Kamu sakitkah?
Don't you feel well?	Kamu tidak sihatkah?
Get well.	Pulih cepat.
He is not well?	Dia kurang sihat?
He doesn't feel well.	Dia berasa kurang sihat.
*I am **sick**.*	Saya **sakit.**
I am not feeling well.	Saya berasa kurang sihat
*I feel **dizzy**.*	Saya berasa **pening**
I have cut my self.	Saya melukakan diri saya
*I have a **burn**.*	Saya **terlecur.**
I need to be examined.	Saya mahu diperiksa.
What hurts?	Apa yang menyakitkan?
I have pain here.	Saya terasa kesakitan di sini.
Where is the pain?	Dimanakah kesakitan itu?
Take rest.	Berehatlah.
When did it start?	Bilakah ini bermula?
After eating.	Selepas makan.
I feel better.	Saya berasa sihat sedikit.
I have stomach ache.	Saya sakit perut.
I think its food poisoning.	Saya mungkin keracunan makanan.
I want to vomit.	Saya hendak muntah.
*I was **sick**.*	Saya telah **sakit**
*She has **pain**.*	Dia berasa **sakit.**
*The lady is **nauseous**.*	Wanita itu berasa **loya**.
*Why are you **not well**?*	Mengapakah kamu **tidak sihat?**

In daily conversations, the word **sakit** is used for *pain, sore* and *sickness*.

SENSES	DERIA / RASA
fragrance	wangi
hearing (v)	kedengaran
odor / smell	bau
sense	rasa
sight / vision	penglihatan / visi
taste (v)	rasa
touch (v)	sentuhan
*It **stinks** (smells bad).*	Ini berbau **busuk**.

BUSINESS TERMINOLOGY	ISTILAH PERNIAGAAN
asset	aset
bank	bank
bankruptcy	kemuflisan
boss	ketua
budget	Belanjawan / bujet
business	perniagaan
cargo	kargo
career	kerjaya
cent	sen
change (money returned)	pertukaran / pulang balik
change (money changer)	mengurup
change (small amount)	wang kecil
cheap	murah
coin	syiling
commerce / trade	komersil
corporation / company	korperasi
credit	kredit
customer	pelanggan
customer service	layanan pelanggan
debt	hutang
debtor	penghutang

deposit	simpanan
discount	diskaun / potong harga
economy	ekonomi
employee	pekerja
employer	majikan
expensive	mahal
export	eksport
fee	yuran / bayaran
import	import
income	gaji / pendapatan
invention	penciptaan
investment	pelaburan
items	barangan
job / work	pekerjaan
loan	pinjaman
lucrative / profitable	lumayan
manager	pengurus
market	pasaran
money	wang / duit
office	pejabat
office building	bangunan pejabat
price / cost / worth	harga / kos / nilai
profession / skill	kerjaya / kemahiran
professional support	sokongan professional
profit	keuntungan
qualifications	kelulusan
quality	mutu / kualiti
receipt	resit
reimbursement	bayaran balik
rent	sewa
salary	gaji
service	perkhidmatan
service charge	caj perkhidmatan

shop	kedai
shopping	beli-belah
shortage	kekurangan
tax	cukai
total	jumlah
trade / commerce	perdagangan / komersil
transfer (monetary)	memindahkan (wang)
value	nilai
valuable	bernilai
withdrawal	keluaran

BUSINESS PHRASES	FRASA PERNIAGAAN
I bought _____	Saya sudah beli _____.
Where can I find a bank?	Di mana ada bank?
I will buy _____	Saya akan beli _____.
You buy _____	Kamu beli _____.
Can you lower the price?	Boleh turunkan sedikit harga?
Do you have ____?	Kamu ada _____?
Final price?	Harga mati?
Give me the change.	Pulangkan pertukaran wang saya.
How much is it?	Ini berapa harga?
*You **owe me** twenty ringgit.*	Kamu **hutang saya** dua puluh ringgit.
I owe you some money.	Saya hutang anda wang.
It is cheap.	Ini murah.
It is expensive.	Ini mahal.
*Will you give me a **discount**?**	Boleh **diskaun**?

* In Malaysia, one can politely request for a discount with the shopowner or the salesperson at the street markets, individual stores at tourists landmarks. It is a trading culture that creates interaction and friendship with the traders and customers.

OCCUPATIONS	PEKERJAAN
What is your job?	Apakah pekerjaan anda?
I am a...	Saya ialah seorang …
actor	pelakon / artis
agent	ejen
architect	arkitek
artist	pelukis
baker	pembuat roti
barber	gunting rambut daging pembina
bartender	pelayan bar
bureaucrat / govt. worker	birokrat / pekerja kerajaan
butcher	penjual daging
builder	Juru bina
businessman / merchant	ahli perniaga
carpenter	tukang kayu
chef	cef / tukang masak
chemist	ahli kimia
construction worker	buruh binaan
consultant / advisor	perunding / penasihat
cook	tukang masak
craftsman	tukang seni
customer service	layanan pelanggan
dancer	penari
dentist	doktor gigi
doctor	doktor
driver	pemandu
electrician	juruelektrik
engineer	jurutera
entrepreneur	usahawan
farmer / peasant	petani
fisherman	nelayan
gardener	tukang kebun

guard	pengawal
hunter	pemburu
interpreter	jurubahasa
judge	hakim
lawyer	peguam
mason	tukang batu
mechanic	mekanik
merchant	saudagar
midwife	bidan
musician	ahli muzik
nurse	jururawat
organizer	penganjur
painter	pelukis
pilot	juruterbang
plumber	tukang paip
politician	ahli politik
professional	professional
prostitute	pelacur
repair man	juru pembaikan
retiree	pesara
salesman	jurujual
secretary	setiausaha
domestic worker	pembantu rumah
servant	pembantu rumah
shepherd	pengembala
singer	penyanyi
shop keeper	pembantu kedai
tailor	tukang jahit
teacher	guru
trainer	pelatih
translator	penterjemah
veterinarian	doktor haiwan
volunteer	sukarelawan

weaver	penenun
worker	pekerja
writer	penulis

EDUCATION	PELAJARAN
answer	jawapan
assignment	tugasan
attention / concentration focus	perhatian / fokus
behavior / character	kelakuan / tingkah laku
book	buku
break / rest	rehat
chalk	kapur tulis
class room	bilik darjah / kelab
class work	kerja kelas
college	kolej
discipline	disiplin
graduation	tamat pengajian
homework	kerja rumah
knowledge	pengetahuan
library	perpustakaan
memorization	penghafalan
notebook	buku nota
page	muka surat
paper	kertas
pen	pen
pencil	pensel
principal	pengetua
question	soalan
school	sekolah
scissors	gunting
strict	tegas
student	pelajar
study (v)	belajar

teach	mengajar
test	ujian
uneducated*	tidak berpendidikan
wisdom	kebijaksanaan
wise	bijak

Phrases	Ayat
What do you study?	Apakah kursus yang kamu ambil?
*What **did** you study?*	Apakah kursus yang **pernah** kamu ambil?
I have a question.	Saya ada satu soalan.
I learned Malay.	Saya telah belajar Bahasa Malaysia.
I will learn Malay.	Saya akan belajar Bahasa Malaysia.
I teach English.	Saya mengajar Bahasa Inggeris.
I tutor in English and Malay.	Saya membimbing dalam Bahasa Inggeris dan Bahasa Melayu.

* When we talk about someone who is *uneducated*, we use a proverb by the direct translated meaning of *alphabet blindness*, which is **buta huruf**.

FIELD OF STUDY	JURUSAN
architecture	arkitek
agriculture	pertanian
art	seni
biology	biologi / kaji hayat
business	perniagaan
chemistry	kimia
communication	komunikasi
design	pereka (n) / rekaan (n) / mereka (v)
economics	ekonomi
engineering	kejuruteraan
English	Bahasa Inggeris
geography	geografi
sociology	sociologi
history	tawarikh / sejarah

law	undang-undang
mathematics	matematik
managment	pengurusan
medicine	perubatan
natural resources	bahan mentah semulajadi
nursing	kejururawatan
philosophy	falsafah
physics	fizik
psychology	psikologi
science	sains
teaching	mengajar

TOOLS	PERKAKAS
axe	kapak
bucket	baldi
hammer	tukul
ladder	tangga
nail	paku
pliers	plier
saw	gergaji
screw	skru
screw driver	pemutar skru
shovel	penyodok
sickle	sabit
wrench	sepana

CONSTRUCTION MATERIAL	BAHAN-BAHAN PEMBINAAN
asphalt	asfalt
brick	bata
ceramic	seramik
completed	siap
concrete (dry)	konkrit (kering)
concrete (wet) - mortar	konkrit (basah) - mortar

construction	pembinaan
bronze	gangsa
copper	tembaga
glass	kaca
glue	gam
gravel	kerikil
metal	logam
pipe	paip
plastic	plastik
rebar	tetulang
rock / stone	batu
sand	pasir
steel	keluli
string	tali
The project is completed	*Projek itu telah selesai.*
The project is not complete.	*Projek itu belum selesai.*

TOURISM	PERLANCONGAN
ascent	daki
backpack	beg galas
backpacker	penggembara
hut	pondok
stopover	persinggahan
peak	puncak
island	pulau
dirt treks	denai tanah
tar roads	Jalan tar
jungle trail	denai hutan
descent	turun
hike	mendaki
hotel	hotel
homesickness	rindu
reservation	tempahan

scenery	pemandang
souvenir	cenderamata
suit case / luggage	bagasi
tour	lawatan
track	Denai / trek
traveler	pelancong
trek(king)	kembara

The beach at Pangkor Island – Andrew Tadross

PHRASES FOR TRAVELLERS	FRASA UNTUK PELANCONG
Show me.	Tunjukkan kepada saya.
Take a picture.	Ambil gambar.
printed photo	gambar tercetak
reminder / souvenir	cenderahati
Can I take your photo?	Bolehkah saya ambil gambar kamu?

Can you show me on map?	Bolehkan tunjukkan tempat it di atas peta?
Have a good trip.	Selamat jalan
It is not far.	Perjalanan tidak jauh.
She feels homesick.	Dia berasa rindu.

TRANSPORT VEHICLES	KENDERAAN
airplane	kapal terbang
bicycle	basikal
boat	bot
bus	bas
car / automobile	kereta / motokar
ferry	feri
light rail transit	transit aliran ringan
monorail	monorail
pickup truck	trak / lori
ship	kapal
taxi	teksi
train	keretapi
transit bus	bas transit
truck	lori
underground trains / transits	keretapi / transit bawah tanah

Christine Mouyon

TRANSPORTATION TERMINOLOGY	ISTILAH KENDERAAN
arrve	tiba
arrival	ketibaan
depart	bertolak / berlepas
departure	perlepasan
destination	perjalanan / destinasi
flight	penerbangan
delay	lewat /terlambat
journey	perjalanan
landing	pendaratan
passenger	penumpang
path	lorong
public transportation	pengangkutan awam
road	jalanraya
short cut	jalan singkat
take off	berlepas

toll road	jalan bertol
touch down	mendarat
traffic	trafik / lalu lintas
traffic jam	kesesakan lalu lintas
transportation	pengangkutan
tunnel	terowong
seat	tempat duduk
slow / slowly	perlahan
stop	berhenti

STATION / TERMINALS	STESEN / TERMINAL
airport	lapangan terbang
bicycle / motorbike parking	lempat letak basikal / motosikal
bus station	stesenbass
car parking	tempat letak kereta / parkir
ferry terminal	terminal feri
helipad	landasan helikopter
highway / expressway	lebuhraya
jetty	jeti
port	pelabuhan
train station / railway station	stesen keretapi
tunnel	terowong
Are there trains to ...	Ada keretapi ke ...?
Are they stops in between?	Ada perhentian di antara perjalanan?
Can we buy return trips from ____ to ____?	Bolehkah kami beli perjalanan pergi-balik dari ____ ke ____?
Do you go to____?	Anda hendak pergi ke____?
How long is the ferry ride?	Berapa lamakah perjalanan feri?
How long is the journey?	Perjalanan mengambil berapa lama?
Is there a space?	Ada cukup tempat / ruang?
Please drive slowly.	Tolong pandu perlahan.
Please stop for us at the next stop.	Tolong berhenti untuk kami bila sampai hentian seterus.
Please stop here / there.	Tolong berhenti di sini / sana.

What time does it arrive?	Waktu apa akan tiba?
What time does it depart?	Waktu apa akan berlepas?

AUTOMOBILE TERMINOLOGY	ISTILAH AUTOMOBIL
automatic	automatik
standard / stick shift	biasa /
brake	brek
break down	rosak
broken	pecah
car	kereta / motokar
car accident	kemalangan jalan raya
car owner	pemilik kereta
crack	retak
dented	kemek
engine	enjin
fast speed	laju
flat tire	tayar pancit
hood	hud
petrol	petrol / minyak
gas station	stesen minyak
motor	motor
speed	kelajuan
tire	tayar
wheel	roda
wind shield	cermin depan

FOOD AND BEVERAGES	MAKANAN DAN MINUMAN
appetite	selera
bill	bil
bowl	mangkuk
bread	roti
breakfast	sarapan
butter	mentega

café	kafe
cake	kek
candy	gula-gula
cheese	keju
cooking oil	minyak masak
carbohydrate	karbohidrat
customer	pelanggan
delicious food	makanan enak /sedap
dinner	makan malam
drink/ beverage	minuman
enough / sufficient	cukup
flour	tepung gandum
food / meal	makanan
fork	garpu
glass	gelas
grill	panggang
honey	madu
hunger	kelaparan
hungry	lapar
knife	pisau
lunch	makan tengahari
napkin	napkin
plate	pinggan
restaurant	restoran
sauce	sos
servant	pembantu
snack	snek
spice	rempah
spoon	sudu
stew	stu
tempe (fermented soyabean cake)	tempeh
tip (gratuity)	tip
vegetarian	makan sayuran / tidak makan daging

protein	protein
waitress / waiter	pelayan
with	dengan
without	tanpa
yogurt	dadih / yogurt
alcohol free	tanpa alkohol
without ice	tanpa ais
with ice	dengan ais
Tea **without** sugar	teh **tanpa** gula

TASTES AND FLAVOURS	RASA DAN PERISA
alkaline water	air alkali / air soda
bitter	pahit
bitter sweet chocolates	coklat pahit manis
bland	tawar
cardamon	pelaga
cinnamon	kulit kayu manis
clove	bunga cengkih
coconut flavour	perisa kelapa
ginger	halia
ginger flower	bunga kantan
green lime flavour	perisa lima hijau
honey	madu
hot and spicy curry	kari pedas dan berempah
jintan manis	aniseed

jintan putih	cumin
lemon flavour	perisa limau kuning
mint flavour	perisa pudina
nutmeg	buah pala
palm sugar	gula melaka
pandan leave /extract	daun pandan
pepper	lada
saffron	safron
salt	garam
salty	masin
sour	masam
spicy (aroma)	berempah
spicy (taste)	pedas
star anise	bunga lawang
sugar	gula
sweet	manis
sweet and sour sauce	sos manis masam
tamarind	asam jawa
tumeric	kunyit
vanilla	vanila
vinegar	cuka

Alcoholic beverages are not encouraged to be served or to be offered to the Malaysian Muslim friends as it is forbidden by the religion. Instead, one may sit in for a coffee, a tea, a juice or even the local dessert drinks and **bubur**, a (sweet dessert).

If a traveller is curious to have a Chinese tea serving and drinking session, look out for a tea house that has proper equipment in Chinese tea brewing techniques. Get to know a few Chinese seniors around the local coffee shops or in tea shops. They are more than happy to disclose their ancient culture of tea drinking to any tourists, especially the young generations. The sit down tea session honours more of the interactions on 'relationship building' or friendship made, and the opportunity of getting to know others from different cultures.

At the Indian eating shops, travellers may try out the Madras fresh milk coffee served in a small drinking vessel. The coffee resembles the western version of *caffé latte*. The smoothness from the slow sips that enters the pallate is a really 'chillout' effect.

BEVERAGES	MINUMAN
alcohol	alkohol
alcohol free	tiada alkohol
beer	bir
bottle	botol
bottle cap opener	pembuka botol
bottled water	air dalam botol
can	tin
coffee	kopi
coffee without milk & sugar	kopi kosong
coffee without milk (with sugar)	kopi- O
cold beer	bir sejuk
cold water	air sejuk
hot coffee	kopi panas
hot water	air panas
iced coffee	kopi ais
juice*	jus
milk	susu
mineral water	air mineral
rice wine (local)	tuak**
soft drink / soda	minuman ringan / soda
tea. 'pulled tea'	teh, the tarik
toddy*** (coconut palm wine)	todi
warm water	air suam
water	air
wine	wain

For fruit juices, just mention the fruit's name follows after the word **jus**. For example, *apple juice* is translated as jus epal.

LOCAL MALAYSIAN BEVERAGES

The Malaysian beverage menu has a variety of localized drinks culture. Local coffee is prepared by adding coarsely ground coffee powder in boiling water and sieved through muslin cloth sieves specially sewn for local Hainanese coffee shops.

Local coffee drinks are served hot or cold. One can have a choice to add sugar only to your coffee, which the locals call it as Kopi-O. Whereas, if you order a black coffee, with no sugar and no milk, it will be called *kopi kosong* , which translates direct as *zero coffee*.

Teh tarik when directly translated means *pulled tea*. It is one of the local milk tea made from ceylonese tea and condensed milk. It is mixed together and then 'pulled' to aerate the milk tea into a smooth bodied drink.

Toddy is coconut palm flower wine that is fermented on the tree. It is a cooling and refreshing alcoholic beverage drank by some locals. It can be an unexpectedly strong beverage due to the fruity mouthfeel of the drink, that is continuously drank as coconut juice.

Tuak is a native rice wine fermented for formal occassions of the native tribes of Sabah and Sarawak. It is a drink served to honour the guests / tourists that visit the long house communities.

BEVERAGES TERMINOLOGY	ISTILAH UNTUK MINUMAN
bottle	botol
bottle cap opener	pembuka kap
bottled water	air botol
can	tin
coffee cup	cawan kopi
coffee pot	teko kopi
cup	cawan
glass	gelas
hot water	air panas
ice-cube	kuib ais
less sugar	sedikit / kurang gula
no sugar	tanpa gula
saucer	piring
sieve	penapis

small bowl	mangkuk kecil
snack	snek / makanan ringan
sugar	gula
tablespoon	sudu besar
teaspoon	sudu teh
to make coffee	buat kopi

PHRASES AND CONVERSATION DURING MEALS.	FRASA DAN PERBUALAN SEMASA MAKAN.
Are you hungry?	Kamu laparkah?
Bring me / Give me this.	Beri saya ini.
Do you like?	Kamu suka?
Do you want this?	Kamu mahu yang inikah?
Give me this / that.	Berikan saya ini / itu.
He does not eat _____.	Dia tidak makan _____.
Here you are (take).	Nah, ambillah.
How much is it?	Ini harganya berapa?
I am full.	Saya sudah kenyang.
I am hungry.	Saya lapar.
I am not hungry.	Saya tidak lapar.
I am thirsty.	Saya dahaga / haus.
I don't like _____	Saya tidak suka _____.
I don't want anything.	Saya tidak mahu apa-apa.
I like _____.	Saya suka _____.
Is there anything to eat?	Ada apa-apa yang boleh dimakan?
Pass me _____.	Ambilkan untuk saya _____.
*She is a **vegetarian**. **	Dia seorang pemakan sayuran.*
tastes good.	Rasanya sedap / enak.
The food here is delicious .	Makanan di sini sedap rasanya.
*This fruit is **bad**.*	Buah ini telah **rosak**.
*The milk has turned **bad**.*	Susu itu sudah **rosak**.
They do not like _____.	Mereka tidak suka _____.
What do you want to drink?	Apakah yang kamu hendak minum?

What do you want?	Apakah yang kamu mahu?
What is there to drink?	Di sana ada apa minuman?
Yes, I like ____.	Ya, Saya suka _____.

*In the above sentence we can also translate that to the opposite form to vegetarian by using '*does not eat meat*' as ' Dia tidak makan daging.' There is not definite word for vegetarian in the Malay cultural context

FOOD / INGREDIENTS	MAKANAN / RAMUAN
beancurd	taufu
beef	daging lembu
bread	roti
buffalo	daging kerbau
cake	kek
candy	kandi
chicken	daging ayam
chilli paste	pes cili
cooking oil	minyak masak
egg	telur
fermented durian paste	tempoyak
fish	ikan
flour	tepung
honey	madu
meat	daging
mutton	daging kambing
paprika	serbuk cili
pepper grain (black)	lada hitam
pepper grain (white)	lada putih
pepper powder	lada sulah
pork	daging babi
salt	garam
salt (rock)	garam batu
seafood	makanan laut
spice	rempah

sugar (brown)	gula perang
sugar (raw)	gula mentah
sugar (rock)	gula batu
sugar (white)	gula putih
venison	daging rusa
vinegar	cuka
yogurt	dadih

FOOD PREPARATION	PENYEDIAAN MAKANAN
bake	membakar
boiled	mendidih
container	bekas
cooking	memasak
delicious	sedap
fresh	segar
fried	menggoreng
grill	panggang
kitchen	dapur
oven	oven
pan	periuk / kuali
pot	periuk
raw	mentah
salted	dengan garam
stove	dapur
spicy (contains spices)	berempah
spicy (taste)	pedas
taste bitter	pahit
taste bland	tawar
taste salty	masin
taste sour	masam
taste sweet	manis
unsalted	tanpa garam

Malaysian herbs and spices. – Mae Cheong

FRUITS	BUAH-BUAHAN
ambra	kedondong
apple	epal
apricot	aprikot
avocado	avokado
banana	pisang
berries	beri
carambola / starfruit	belimbing besi
durian	durian
fig	buah ara
grapes	anggur
guava	jambu batu
lemon	limau
lime (green)	limau hijau
lime (kaffir)	limau purut
lime (musk) / calamansi	limau kasturi
mandarin orange	limau mandarin
mango	mangga
mangosteen	manggis
orange	oren
papaya	betik
passionfruit	buah markisa
peach	pic

pear	pir
raisin	raisin
rambutans	rambutan
rose apple	jambu air
sugar dates	kurma
watermelon	tembikai

VEGETABLES	**SAYUR-SAYURAN**
bean / pea	kekacang
beets	beet
cabbage	kubis
carrot	lobak merah
chickpea	kacang kuda
coriander	ketumbar
corn / maize	biji jagung / jagung
eggplant	terung
french beans	kacang buncis
garlic	bawang putih
greenpeas	kacang hijau
horseradish	lobak putih
lentils	dahl
lettuce	daun salad
long beans	kacang panjang
mushroom	cendawan
okra	bendi
olive	zaitun
onion	bawang merah
peanut / groundnut	kacang tanah
pepper	lada
potato	ubi kentang
pumpkin	buah labu
red chilli	cili merah
sago (palm bark)	sagu

small chilli	cili padi
spinach	bayam
sweet potato	ubi keledek
tapioca / cassava	ubi kayu
tomato	tomato
water convolulus	kangkung
yam	ubi keladi

GRAINS	BIJIRIN
barley	barli
cooked rice	nasi
cous-cous	kas-kas
dahl	kacang dal
oats	oat
rice	beras
sago	sagu
sorghum	sorghum
wheat	gandum

ANIMAL TERMS	ISTILAH HAIWAN
animal	binatang / haiwan
endangered species	spesis terancam
endemic species	spesis endemik
extinct species	spesis pupus
feather	pelepah
fish	ikan
hoof	kaki
horn	tanduk
livestock	ternakan
mammal	mamalia
mating	pengawanan
reptile	reptilia
slaughter (v)	menyembelih
species	spesis

udder	kelenjar susu
wool	bulu biri-biri

DOMESTIC ANIMALS	HAIWAN JINAK
bird	burung
buffalo	kerbau
calf	anak lembu
camel	unta
cat	kucing
cattle	lembu
chicken	ayam
cow	lembu
dog	anjing
donkey	keldai
duck	itik
fighting fish	ikan pelaga
goat	kambing
goose	angsa
guinea pig	tikus belanda
horse	kuda
kitten	anak kucing
mouse / rat	tikus
ox	lembu jantan
peacock	merak
pet	haiwan kesayangan
pig	babi
pony	kuda padi
puppy	anak anjing
quail	puyuh
rabbit	arnab
sheep / lamb	biiri-biri
turkey	ayam belanda

WILD ANIMALS	HAIWAN LIAR
baboon	babun
bat	kelawar
beetle	kumbang
butterfly	rama-rama
centipede	lipan
chimpazee	chimpazee
cobra	ular tedung
crocodile	buaya
deer	rusa
dolphin	ikan lumba-lumba
dugong (manatee)	dugong
eagle	helang
elephant	gajah
flying fox	kelawar besar
fox	musang
giraffe	zirafah
gorilla	gorila
grasshopper	belalang
leopard	harimau bintang
lion	singa
millipede	gonggok
monitor lizard	biawak
monkey	monyet
moth	kupu-kupu
mousedeer	kancil
orang utan	orang utan
ostrich	burung unta
python	ular sawa
rabbit	arnab
snake	ular
spider	labah-labah
tapir	tenuk

tiger	harimau
tortoise	kura-kura
turtle	penyu
whale	paus
whale / shark	jerung
wild cat	kucing hutan
wildebeest	seladang
wolf	serigala
zebra	kuda belang

SMALL ANIMALS	HAIWAN KECIL
ant	semut
bat	kelawar
bee	lebah
bird	burung
dragonfly	pepatung
earthworm	cacing
flea	kutu
fly	lalat
frog	katak
insect	serangga
lice	kutu
lizard	cicak
locust	belalang besar
mosquito	nyamuk
snail	siput babi
spider	labah-labah
toad	kodok
tortoise	kura-kura
worm	ulat

FARMING	PERLADANGAN
agriculture	pertanian
agro-forestry	pertanian-perhutanan
animal enclosure	kandang
cow dung	tahi lembu
crop	tanaman
dry land	tanah kering
farm	kebun
farmland	kawasan ladang
fertile	subur
fertiliser	baja
garden	taman / kebun bunga
grazing field	padang ragut
irrigation	saliran
orchard	dusun
paddy field	sawah
seed	benih
top soil	tanah atas
yield / harverst	tuaian

EVENTS (PERAYAAN)

Malaysia is a multiethnic society. Hence we celebrate quite a few festivals as the seasons pass. Traditional food of each ethnic group will be served during festivities.

Muslims celebrate the **Eid** celebration after fasting for a month in Ramadhan. During the fasting period, the Muslims will break fast from dusk and they can eat until dawn, before sunrise. The Eid celebration lasts for a month during which guests and relatives will visit to the Muslim homes. The Malay traditional foods are **rendang, lemang, ketupat**, pressed rice, spicy beef floss and sweet dessert called **bubur lampok**.

The **Aidil Adha** celebration is celebrated after the pilgrimage to Mecca and with the sacrificing of cows and goats for meat to the needy.

The Hindus celebrate **Deepavali, Ponggal** and **Thaipusam**. Special traditional food will be served during the celebrations. Some Hindus will practice vegetarianism during these auspicious events.

Easter celebration is a Christian tradition. Christians also celebrate Christmas. Some of the native people in the country are Christians too.

The mid-autumn festival is celebrated by the Chinese community around the month of September. During this auspicious day, family members and friends gather together for a reunion to savour various types of mooncakes, snacks and Chinese tea drinking.

During the Chinese Winter Solstice Festival, a sweet dessert made of colourful glutinous rice balls is served after a family meal.

Approximately about a month after the Winter Solstice Festival, the Lunar New Year enters celebration which is traditionally lasting for 15 days. At those times, each day holds a festival which is observed by different dialects of the Chinese community present in this country.

The Harvest Festival or **Hari Ka'amatan** is celebrated by the Kadazan -dusun and Murut tribes of Sabah, as a gesture of thanksgiving dedicated to the Rice Gods. Agricultural shows, buffalo races, and traditional games are events held. Other events include much merrymaking and feasting with rice wine (**tuak**) throughout the festivities. The natives dress in their traditional costumes and enjoy a carnival atmosphere which stretches from daybreak till dawn.

The **Gawai Dayak** is usually held on the first and second day of June. After the farmers have harvested their grains, villagers gather in longhouses and offer a thanksgiving and invoke blessings for the following harvest. The natives have a fiest and serve rice wine, as the most essential part of the meal. The rice wine is also offered to the gods during ceremonies.

HOLIDAYS	CUTI
birthday	harijadi
celebration	perayaan
Chinese New Year	Tahun Baru Cina
Chinese Spring Festival	Perayaan Musim Bunga Cina
Christmas	Hari Natal / Krismas
culture	budaya

Easter	Paskah
Eid celebration	Hari Raya Aidil Fitri
feast	jamuan besar
Gawai Festival	Hari Gawai
gift	hadiah / buah tangan
Haj celebration	Hari Raya Haji / Qurban
mid-Autumn festival	Perayaan Tanglung
New Year	Tahun Baru
season	musim
tradition	tradisi
Happy birthday	Selamat Hari Jadi
Happy Easter	Paskah
happy holiday	selamat bercuti
Merry Christmas	Selamat Hari Natal

RELIGION	**AGAMA**
Animism	Animisma
Buddhism	Buddha
Catholic	Katholik
Christian	Kristian
Hinduism	Hindu
Judaism	Yahudi
Methodist	Methodist
Muslim	Muslim
Protestant	Protestan
Taoism	Tao

RELIGIOUS TERMINOLOGY	**ISTILAH KEAGAMAAN**
ancient	kuno
angel	malaikat
belief / trust	kepercayaan
Bible	kitab injil
church	gereja

cross / crucifix	salib
fasting	berpuasa
forgiveness	berampun maaf
God	Tuhan
heaven / paradise	syurga
hell	neraka
hindu temple	kuil
holy /sacred	suci
Islamic	Islam
Jesus	Nabi Isa
monastery	biara
moral	moral / akhlak
morality	kemoralan
mosque	masjid
myth / story / legend	legenda
orthodox	ortodoks
philosophy	falsafah
priest	sami, imam, pastor
religion	agama
satan	setan
sin	dosa
spirit	roh

The term *priest* used in English when applies to different religions in the country, different Malay words are specifically used for the respectively as in different religions; **sami** is for Hindus and Buddhists, **imam** is for Muslims and **pastor** is for Christians.

GOVERNMENT	KERAJAAN
administration	pentadbiran
association / union	persatuan
authority / power	pihak berkuasa
campaign	kempen

capitalism	kapitalisma
chairman	pengerusi
communism	komunisma
conflict	konflik
corruption	rasuah
democracy	demokrasi
dictator	diktator
district	daerah
election	pilihanraya
king	raja
leader	pemimpin
leadership	kepimpinan
mayor	dato bandar
monarchy	kerabat
NGO	Organisasi bukan kerajaan
politics	politik
prohibited	dilarang
propaganda	propaganda
queen	permaisuri
regime	regim
regulation	undang-undang
respect	hormat
royalty	diraja
socialism	sosialisma
speech	pengumuman
stability	kestabilan
the main issue	isu utama
tyrant	zalim
vote	undi / pilih
voter	pengundi
zone	kawasan

SOCIETY	MASYARAKAT
anarchy	anarki
crowd	orang ramai
demonstration (peaceful)	demostrasi aman
discrimination	diskriminasi
equality	kesaksamaan
freedom / liberty	kebebasan
freedom of speech	kebebasan bersuara
group	kumpulan
human	manusia
humanity	kemanusiaan
human rights	hak kemanusiaan
ignorance	kejahilan
individual	individu / perseorangan
inequality	ketidaksaksamaan
injustice	tidak adil
justice	kezaliman
labor	buruh
orphan	yatim
orphanage	rumah yatim
people	orang
population	penduduk
protest	membangkang
protester	pembangkang
racism	perkauman
revolution	revolusi
riot / disturbance	rusuhan / gangguan
rich / poor	kaya / miskin
segregation	perbelahan
sexism	seksis
stereotype	stereotaip

MEDIA	MEDIA
argument	pergaduhan
controversial	kontroversial

controversy	kontroversi
debate	bahas
events	peristiwa
film / movie	filem
issue	isu
journalist / reporter	wartawan
magazine	majalah
mass media	media massa
news	berita
newspaper	surat khabar / akhbar
scandal	skandal
truth / honest	jujur

Malaysians are made up of a very diverse ethinicity. The colourful events, their beliefs, the cultural norms, the art and the food savoured reflect a big meaning about her cultural diversities to tourists and people who come to work in this country.

The citizens celebrate different cultural and religious events along with other ethnic communities every season. We enjoy much of the delicious and colourful meals served by the respective cultures. Tourists and foreign residence are not left out in most of these events as the locals welcome them to have an experience of 'family reunions' while they are away from their homelands.

Due to the communial aspects, the close-knit societal environments in most communities, our intercultural awareness and the manners in varied cultural interactions are important for us to observe. We are sensitive in respecting and in tolerating our various cultural interactions to maintain harmonious living. Tourists and foreign residents who arrive shortly may experience our friendliness and helpful senses. Our smiles are inexpensive to offer. So for a good hint to the tourists and newcomers, do return a smile and greet each other along your travel and stay. The locals are delighted to hear tourists or foreigners greeting them in the native Malay way, **Apa khabar?**

SOCIAL ISSUES	ISU-ISU SOSIAL
addict (person)	penagih dadah
alcoholic	alkoholik
bad habit	tabiat buruk

beggar	pengemis
charity	amal
child labour	buruh kanak-kanak
cigarette	rokok
depression	kemurungan
donation	derma
drug	dadah
drunk	mabuk
gambling	berjudi
hangover	mabuk
homeless	orang jalanan / gelangdangan
illiteracy	buta huruf
inequality	ketidaksaksamaan
infant mortality	kadar kematian bayi
insane / crazy	gila / tidak siuman
mental health	kesihatan mental
poor	miskin
poverty	kemiskinan
prostitution	pelacuran
rich	kaya
suicide	bunuh diri
unemployed (adj/noun)	menganggur
unemployment	pengangguran

CRIME	JENAYAH
burglary	kecurian
child abuse	penderaan kanak-kanak
criminal	penjenayah
dead	mati / meninggal dunia
death	kematian
domestic abuse	keganasan domestik
fraud	penipuan
guilt	salah
inmate / prisoner	banduan

innocent	tidak bersalah
killer	pembunuh
murder	pembunuhan
police	polis
police station	balai polis
prison	penjara / jail
prisoner	banduan
rape	rogol
robbery	rompakan
sexual abuse	keganasan seksual
shooting	tembak-menembak
thief	pencuri
threat	ancaman / ugutan
vandalism	vandalisma
victim	mangsa
violence	keganasan

LEGAL TERMS — ISTILAH UNDANG-UNDANG

bribe	rasuah
contract	perjanjian / kontrak
court	makhamah
guilty	salah
innocent	tidak bersalah
illegal	haram / tidak sah
legal	sah
law	undang-undang
lawyer /advocate	peguam
penalty	denda
punishment	hukuman
rule	peraturan
trial	perbicaraan
unjust	tidak adil
violation	kesalahan

TERMINOLOGY FOR IMMIGRATION	ISTILAH IMIGRESEN
adoption	pengambilan
application	permohonan / aplikasi
birth date	tarikh lahir
birthplace	tempat lahir
cheap labour	buruh murah
citizen	warganegara
colony	koloni
customs office	pejabat kastam
ethnicity	etnik
flag	bendera
foreigner	orang asing
foreign aid	pertologan asing
identification	pengesahan
immigrant	pendatang
immigration	imigresen
language	bahasa
national	kebangsaan
nationality	kewarganegaraan
race	bangsa
signature	tandatangan
surname	nama keluarga
visa / passport	visa / pasport
xenophobia	xenofobia

CONVERSATIONS	PERBUALAN
Where are you from?	Kamu dari mana?
I from American	**Saya dari** Amerika.
I come from _____.	**Saya datang** dari _____.
I live in _____.	Saya tinggal di _____.
*What is your **nationality**?*	Apakah kewarganegaraan anda?
I am an Egyptian.	**Saya orang** Mesir.
She is a/ an _____ *(nationality)*	**Dia orang** _____.

*What language **do you speak?***	Kamu boleh **berbahasa** apa?
***I can speak** in English.*	**Saya boleh bertutur** dalam Bahasa Inggeris
*He can speak **a little bit** of Malay.*	Dia boleh bertutur **sedikit** Bahasa Melayu.
I / We / He understand(s).	Saya / Kami / Dia faham.
*Sorry, can you speak **slower?***	Maaf, boleh anda cakap **perlahan sedikit**?
*My **surname** is Musa.*	**Nama keluarga saya** Musa.

CONFLICT	KONFLIK
ally	sekutu
ammunition	peluru
army	tentera
battle	peperangan
bomb	bom
bullet	peluru
combat (fighting)	pertarungan
coup d'état	rampasan kuasa
chaos	huru-hara
enemy	musuh
explosive material	bahan letupan
genocide	pembunuhan beramai-ramai
gun	senapang
hatred	kebencian
invasion	serangan
military / soldier	tentera / askar
peace	keamanan
pistol	pistol
reconciliation	perdamaian
slavery	perhambaan
struggle	perjuangan
sword	pedang
terrorism	keganasan
terrorist	pengganas
torture	seksa

victory	kemenangan
war	perang
weapon	senjata
world peace	keamanan dunia

CONVERSATION BY PHONE	**PERBUALAN MELALUI TELEFON**
Call me.	Tolong panggil / telefon saya.
Can I call you?	Bolehkah saya panggil / telefon kamu?
Can I talk to _____?	Bolehkah saya bercakap dengan ?
Hold just a minute.	Tolong tunggu sebentar.
I am in ..._____.	Saya di …
I called you.	Saya telah menelefon kamu.
I can't hear you.	Saya tidak dapat dengar kamu.
I didn't hear you.	Saya tidak dengar kamu.
I left a message.	Saya tinggalkan pesanan.
I will call you.	Saya akan telefon kamu.
I'm talking on the phone.	Saya sedang bercakap di telefon.
There was no answer.	Tidak ada orang jawab.
Who is speaking?	Siapakah yang bercakap?
What did you say?	Anda berkata apa?

URBAN GEOGRAPHY	**GEOGRAFI PERBANDARAN**
bridge	jambatan
building	bangunan
capital city	ibu kota
city	kota / bandaraya
city center (downtown)	pusat bandaraya
community	komuniti
demographics	demografi
density	kepadatan
development	pembangunan
dweller / resident	penduduk / penghuni
factory	kilang
gutter	longkang

market	pasar
monument	tugu / monumen
neighborhood	kejiranan
park	taman rekreasi
place / location	tempat / lokasi
petrol station	stesen minyak
port	pelabuhan
rural	pendalaman / luar bandar
shopping center	pusat beli-belah
society / community	masyarakat / komuniti
side walk	pejalan kaki
slaughter house	pusat penyembelihan
suburb	pinggir bandar
station	stesen
train	keretapi
urban	bandar
urban plan	pelan perbandaran
warehouse / godown	gudang
village	kampung
villager	orang kampung / penduduk kampung

ACCIDENT	KEMALANGAN
alive	hidup
ambulance	ambulans
broken	patah
damaged	rosak
coffin	keranda
collision	berlanggar
corpse / dead body	mayat
dangerous	bahaya
dead	mati
death	kematian
emergency	kecemasan

funeral	pengebumian
injury	kecederaan
life	nyawa
passenger	penumpang
safe	selamat
tomb / grave	kubur
tragedy	tragedy / kemalangan
tragic	malang
urgent	mustahak

START / FINISH	MULA / TAMAT
final	akhir
The end	tamat
At first	pada mula
beginner	pemula
beginning	permulaan
Almost finished	hampir tamat / hampir selesai
Are you finished? (m)	Kamu sudah selesaikah?
Are you finished? (f)	Kamu sudah selesaikah?
I am not finished.	Saya belum selesai
Is it finished?	Adakah ini selesai?
Not finished.	Belum selesai
I began ...	Saya telah bermula …
I begin ...	Saya bermula …
The first time	Kali pertama
The last time	Kali terakhir

SPORTS	SUKAN
against	melawan / bertanding
athlete	atlit /ahli sukan
audience	pendengar
ball	bola
basketball	bola keranjang
coach	juru latih

champion	juara
endurance	ketahanan
football (soccer)	bola sepak
fan	peminat
favourite team (who is your)	pasukan kegemaran
game	permainan / pertandingan
goal	gol
kick (imperative)	sepak
marathon	marathon
onlookers / spectators	penonton
opponent	pasukan lawan
penalty	penalti
player	pemain
practice / exercise	berlatih / bersenam
referee	pengadil
runner	pelari
score	markah / skor
sport	sukan
stadium	stadium
stamina	kelazakan
swimming	renang
team	pasukan
tie	seri
World Cup	Piala Dunia
wrestling	tinju

Conversation	**Perbualan**
Do you play football?	Kamu main bola sepakkah?
Yes, we do.	Ya, kami bermain bola sepak.
*Do you **watch** the World Cup?* *Yes, can we* go **to watch** that together?*	Adakah anda **tonton** Piala Dunia? Ya, bolehkah kita* pergi **menonton** bersama-sama?
*I **watch** football at the stadium.*	Saya **tengok** bola sepak di stadium.
Who are you a fan of?	Kamu peminat siapa?

Malaysia vs Thailand	Malaysia **lawan** Thailand
Who is playing?	Siapakah yang bermain?
Who is your favorite team?	Yang manakah pasukan kegemaran anda?

*When you watch an event on a screen use the verb **tonton or menonton** to represent the action of *watch*. When you watch a game or event in the location, you use the verb **tengok**.

COMPETITION	PERTANDINGAN
1st	pertama
2nd	kedua
3rd	ketiga
gold	emas
silver	perak
bronze	gangsa
advantage	kebaikan
average	purata, sederhana
better	lebih baik
best	terbaik
effort	minat
loser	yang kalah
prize / award	hadiah / anugerah
winner	pemenang
bad (situation, attitude)	tidak baik (keadaan, kelakuan)
worse	teruk
worst	sangat teruk
*He is **better**.*	Dia **lebih baik**.
*You are the **best**.*	Kamulah yang **terbaik**.
*It is the **worst**.*	Ini yang **terteruk**.

WEATHER	IKLIM
season	musim
autumn	musim luruh
spring	musim bunga

summer	musim panas
winter	musim sejuk
cloud / cloudy	awan / berawan / mendung
cold / cool	sejuk / nyaman
condition	keadaan
drought	kemarau
dry	kering / kontang
dry season	musim kering
fog	kabus
hazy	jerebu
heat	kepanasan / bahang
high / strong wind	angin kencang
hot	panas
humid	lembap
humidity	kelembapan
ice	ais
light rain shower	hujan renyai-renyai / gerimis
lightning	kilat
moisture	kelembapan
overcast	mendung
rain	hujan
rainbow	pelangi
rainy season	tengkujuh
smog	kabus
storm	ribut
sunlight	sinaran matahari
sunny	cerah
sunrise	matahari terbit
sunset	matahari terbenam
temperature	suhu
thunder	guruh
tropical	tropika
warm	suam

waves	gelombang
weather	cuaca
windy	berbayu
*It is **sunny**.*	**Keadaan cerah.** (Lit. Condition sunny).
It is a cloudy day.	Keadaan mendung. / Hari ini mendung.
The weather is bad.	Cuaca tidak baik.

IN THE HOUSE	DI DALAM RUMAH
At ___ house.	Di rumah ____.
bed	katil
bedroom	bilik tidur
bench	bangku
broom	penyapu
carpet / rug	permaidani
ceiling	siling
chair	kerusi
compound	halaman
curtain	langsir
desk	meja kecil
door	pintu
drawer	laci
enclosure / fence	pagar
floor	lantai

furniture	perabot
hut	pondok
house	rumah
house work	kerja rumah
inside / interior	di dalam / dalaman
key / lock	kunci
kitchen	dapur
land holder	pemilik tanah
land lord / renter	tuan tanah / tuan rumah
living room	ruang tamu
mansion	banglo
outside / erxterior	di luar / luaran
owner	pemilik / tuan punya
possession	pemilikan
property	harta
rental house	rumah sewa
roof	bumbung
room	bilik / kamar
shelf	rak
stairs	tangga
stool	bangku
store room	bilik stor
table	meja
telephone	telefon
wall	dinding
window	tingkap
yard (back)	halaman (belakang)

BATHROOM	**BILIK MANDI**
blade (razor)	pisau cukur
bath tub	tab mandi
cold water	air sejuk
comb	sikat

warm water	air suam
hot water	air panas
mirror	cermin
plumbing	sistem paip
shower	pancuran mandi
sink	singki
soap	sabun
toilet	tandas
toilet paper	tisu tandas
tooth paste	ubat gigi
toothbrush	berus gigi
towel	tuala
water	air
wet / moist	lembap

SLEEP	**TIDUR**
dream / dreaming	mimpi / bermimpi
nap (short sleep)	berehat sebentar
alarm clock	jam berloceng
blanket	selimut
carpet / rug	permaidani / kain buruk
insomnia	insomia
mattress	tilam
nightmare	mimpi ngeri
overnight	semalaman
pillow	bantal
sheet	cadar
sleepy	mengantuk
snoring (v)	berdengkur
Are you tired?	Kamu letihkah?
*I feel **tired**.*	Saya berasa **letih**.
***I don't feel** tired.*	**Saya tidak** berasa letih.
*She is **sleepy**.*	Dia **mengantuk**.

*They are not sleepy **yet**.*   Mereka **belum** mengantuk lagi.

CLOTHING	PAKAIAN
belt	tali pinggang
bra	baju dalam
clothesline	ampaian
cotton	kapas
dress (female)	baju perempuan
fashion/style	fesyen / gaya
huge	bersaiz besar
laundry	cucian
leather	kulit
lingerie	pakaian dalam
loose	longgar
material/ cloth	fabric / kain
narrow	sempit
new clothes	pakaian baru
old clothes	pakaian lama
pants	seluar panjang
shirt (male)	baju lelaki
shoes	kasut
size	saiz
skirt	skirt

sock	sarung kaki
suit	sut
tight	ketat
too big	terlalu besar
too small	terlalu kecil
underpants	seluar dalam
wide	lebar

FASHION ACCESSORIES	AKSESSORI FESYEN
wrist watch	jam tangan
bracelet	gelang tangan
braids	tocang
cosmetics / makeup	kosmetik / solekan
diamond	berlian
earing	anting-anting
eye glasses	cermin mata
hat	topi
jewel	permata
jewelry	barang kemas
neck tie	tali leher
necklace	rantai leher
sack / bag	beg
perfume	minyak wangi
purse (women's)	dompet (wanita)
ring	cincin
wallet (men's)	dompet (lelaki)

Conversations	Perbualan
*What are you **wearing**?*	Apakah yang anda **pakai**?
*I am **wearing** yellow pants.*	Saya **memakai** seluar kuning.
*I will **wear** white socks.*	Saya akan **pakai** sarung kaki putih.
*I'm **wearing** a red shirt.*	Saya sedang **memakai** baju merah.
*I'm **wearing** black shoes.*	Saya **memakai** kasut hitam.

*He is **wearing** brown pants.*   Dia **memakai** seluar coklat.

The prefix **me-** has to be added to **pakai** to show the transitive action of *wearing*. If the phrase is a command or instruction **pakai** is used directly.

ELECTRICITY / POWER	TENAGA ELETRIK / TENAGA
bright	cerah
charcoal	arang
dark	gelap
electric wire	wayar elektrik
gas	gas
hydroelectric power	tenaga electrik hidro
kerosene	minyak tanah
lamp	lampu
light	lampu
light bulb	mentol lampu
power outage	gangguan bekalan elektrik
power station / plant	stesen janakuasa elektrik
public utilities	perkhidmatan awam
solar power	tenaga solar
switch	suis
wind power	tenaga angin
Turn it on.	Pasang suis.
Turn it off.	Tutup suis.

WATER RESOURCES	PUNCA-PUNCA AIR
contaminated / polluted	kontaminasi / tercemar
dam	empangan
drinking water	air minuman
drainage	saliran
ground water	air bawah tanah
hose	hos
plumbing	sistem paip
pump	pam

spring/water source	airmata / punca air
tap water	air paip
water	air
water pump	pam air
water supply	air bekalan
well	perigi
reservoir	empangan

POSTAL	**POS**
address	alamat
box	peti surat
contact number of receiver	nombor telefon penerima
sender	penghantar
receiver	penerima
town	bandar
city	bandaraya
country	negara
envelope / mail	sampul surat / surat / mel
letter	surat
message	pesanan
package	bungkusan
post code	kod pos
stamp (postage)	setem
state	negeri
street name	nama jalan

*I want to send this **package**.*	Saya mahu hantar **bungkusan** ini.
I am waiting for a package.	Saya sedang menunggu bungkusan saya.
Has my package arrived?	Sudahkah bungkusan saya sampai?

THE WORLD	**DUNIA**
atmosphere	atmosfera
ground/land	tanah
moon	bulan
planet	planet

sky	langit
star	bintang
sun	matahari
universe / outer space	cakarawala / angkasa lepas

DIRECTIONS / LOCATION	FRASA ARAH / LOKASI
here / from here	sini / dari sini
there / to there	sana / dari sana
far	jauh
near	dekat
east	timur
west	barat
north	utara
south	selatan
Cross the road.	Lintas jalan itu.
Go this way.	Pergi arah ini.
I am taking a walk.	Saya sedang bersiar-siar.
To the left.	Belok kiri.
To the right	Belok kanan.
Straight ahead	Jalan terus.
Up there.	Di atas sana.
Down there.	Di bawah sini.
Where are you going?	Kemanakah kamu pergi?
Where are you?	Dimanakah kamu berada?
Near the junction	Dekat simpang jalan.
Over there / here	Di sana / di sini.
***Drive** southward.*	**Pandu** arah selatan.
*Walk **westward**.*	Jalan **arah ke barat.**
I'm taking a walk there.	Saya sedang bersiar-siar di sana.
This way.	Di sini.
Where are you going?	Ke manakah anda pergi?
Where are you?	Di mana kamu berada?
Where is it located?	Di mana lokasinya?

GEOGRAPHY	GEOGRAFI
altitude / elevation	ketinggian
border / limit	sempadan / had
border / edge / boundary	sempadan
continent	benua
country	negara
direction	arah
equator	khatulistiwa
latitude	garisan lintang
local	tempatan
location / place	lokasi / tempat
longitude	garisan bujur
map	peta
region	wilayah

Tea plantations at Cameron Highlands. – Andrew Tadross

GEOLOGY	GEOLOGI
cave	gua
downhill	turun bukit
erosion	hakisan

flat	rata
highland	tanah tinggi
hill	bukit
hole	lubang
hole (deep)	lubang dalam
hole (shallow)	lubuk
land	tanah
lowland	tanah pamah / tanah rendah
mine (gold)	lombong (emas)
mineral	galian
mountain	gunung
mountain peak / apex	puncak gunung
mud	lumpur
pile	longgok
rocky	berbatu-batang
sand	pasir
semi high land	kawasan sederhana tinggi
slope	lereng / cerun bukit
soil	tanah
steep	curam
stone	batu
topography	topografi
underground	bawah tanah
uphill	naik bukit

BODIES OF WATER	**BADAN-BADAN BERAIR**
beach	persisiran pantai
cliff	tebing tinggi
creek / stream	anak sungai
deep water	air dalam
desert	padang pasir
forest	hutan
fresh water	air tawar

grassland	padang rumput
highland	tanah tinggi
island	pulau
lake	tasik
marshland. wetland	kawasan paya
peninsula	semenanjung
pond	kolam
reservoir	empangan
river	sungai
salt water	air masin
shallow water	air cetek
swamp	paya
swift current	arus deras
tropical jungle	hutan tropika
waterfall	air terjun

Siew Li Yap

DISASTER	BENCANA
ash	abu
burn (v)	bakar
collapse (failure)	runtuhan
destroy	rosak

disaster prevention	pencegahan bencana
drainage	saliran
earthquake	gempa bumi
fire (v), fire (n)	kebakaran, api
flame	api
flood	banjir
hazardous / dangerous	bahaya
hurricane	taufan
monsoon	monsun
natural disaster	bencana alam
rescue	selamatkan
smoke	asap
volcano	gunung berapi
catastrophy	malapetaka
Are you scared?	Kamu takut?
I am scared.	Saya takut.

COUNTRY NAMES	NAMA NEGARA
Asia (continent)	Asia (benua)
America	Amerika
Australia	Australia
Bangladesh	Bangladesh
Brazil	Brazil
Cambodia	Kemboja
Canada	Kanada
China	China (chin-na)
Egypt	Mesir
England	England
France	Perancis
Germany	Germany
Greece	Greek
India	India
Indonesia	Indonesia

Israel	Israel
Italy	Itali
Jamaica	Jamaica
Japan	Japan
Kenya	Kenya
Korea	Korea
Netherlands	Belanda
Nigeria	Nigeria
Poland	Poland
Russia	Russia
Saudi arabia	Arab saudi
Singapore	Singapura
Sweden	Sweden
Thailand	Negara Thai
Vietnam	Vietnam

* For nationality, just add the word **orang** or **warga** in front of the country.

> e.g.   Singaporean – **orang** Singapura
> Jordanian – **warga** Jordan

ENVIRONMENT	ALAM
barren	tandus
biodiversity	biodiversiti
climate change	perubahan iklim
conservation	pemuliharaan
consumption	penggunaan
desert	gurun
ecosystem	ekosistem
environment	alam
environmental resources	sumber alam
forest	hutan
forestry	perhutanan
garbage	sampah-sarap

lumber	balak
log	balak
deforestation	penerokaan hutan
reforestation	penanaman semula hutan
man-made	buatan manusia
natural	semulajadi
natural resource	sumber semulajadi
pollution	pencemaran
seedling	anak benih
tree nursery	tapak semaian pokok
habitat	habitat
sustainable	mampan
wildlife	hidupan liar
wilderness	hutan
wildfire	kebakaran hutan
wood	kayu

Mae Cheong

PLANTS	TUMBUHAN
banana plant	pohon pisang
bouganvillae	bunga kertas

branch	dahan
bush / shrub	lalang
cocoa	koko
coconut tree	pokok kelapa
eucalyptus	pokok kayu putih
flower	bunga
frangipani flower	bunga cempaka
fruit tree	pokok buah
grass	rumput
hibiscus scrub	bunga raya
jasmine flower	bunga melur
leaf	daun
marigold	bunga tahi ayam
moss	lumut
oil palm	pokok kelapa sawit
pinang palm	areca nut tree
pine tree	pokok pain
plant	pokok / pohon
root	akar
rubber tree (Hevea brasiliensis)	pokok getah
stem	batang
sunflower	bunga matahari
thorn	duri
tree	pokok
trunk	batang
vine / climber	tumbuhan pemanjat
weed	lalang

Rafflesia Flower – Mae Cheong

MATHEMATICS & SCIENCE	MATEMATIK & SAINS
add	campur
analysis	analsis
chemical	kimia
divide	bahagi
equal	sama dengan
equals	bersamaan
gas	gas
liquid	cecair
fluid	bendalir
math	kira-kira
multiply / times	darab / kali
organic	organik
percent	peratus
physical	fisikal
powder	tepung
ratio	nisbah
scientific	saintifik
solid	pepejal
subtract / minus	tolak

SHAPE / MEASUREMENT	BENTUK / UKURAN
100 kilos	seratus kilogram
amount	jumlah

angle	sudut
area	luas , kawasan
arrow	penunjuk ($\rightarrow$)
center	pusat
circle	bulatan
corner	sudut
curve	lingkungan
depth	kedalaman
distance	jarak
dot/point	titik
elevation / altitude	ketinggian
height	tinggi
infinity ∞	infiniti
insufficient / shortage	tidak mencukupi / kekurangan
length	panjang
line	garis
linear	linear / lurus
measurement	ukuran
more than enough	mencukupi
radius	jejari
rectangle	segi empat
round	bulat
shape	bentuk
square	segi empat sama
triangle	segi tiga
volume	isipadu
weight	berat
width	lebar

LANGUAGE	BAHASA
accent	loghat
adjective	kata adjektif / sifat nama
adverb	kata adverb / sifat kata

alphabet / script	huruf
antonym	antonym / lawan erti
comma	koma
definition	definisi
dictionary	kamus
foreign language	bahasa asing
grammar	tata bahasa
meaning/translation	makna / translasi
noun	kata nama
paragraph	perenggan
plural	jamak
preposition	kata sendi
pronunciation	sebutan
question mark	tanda tanya
sentence	ayat
spelling	ejaan
synonym	sininim / sama erti
verb	kata kerja

PERSONAL DESCRIPTION	SIFAT INDIVIDU
attractive	menarik
beautiful	cantik / molek
handsome	tampan / segak
sexy	seksi
bald	botak
dark (skin)	kulit gelap
dark (hair)	rambut mayang
elderly	tua
elders	tertua
fair (complexion)	cerah
fat / obese	gemuk / kegemukan
gray hair	uban
naked	bogel
old	tua / berusia

old man	lelaki tua
short	pendek / rendah
tall	tinggi
long	panjang
slim	langsing
thin	kurus
ugly	hodoh
young	muda

Andrew Tadross

POSITIVE DESCRIPTION	GAMBARAN POSITIF
accurate	tepat
alert / active	sedar / aktif
astonishing	menakjubkan
beautifull	cantik / molek
brave	gagah / berani
calm	tenang
charisma	karisma
challenging	mencabar

clever	bijak / cerdik
comfortable	selesa
curious	ingin tahu
dependable / reliable	boleh dipercayai
determined	menentu
diligent	rajin
educated	berpelajaran / terpelajar
effective	berkesan
efficient	cekap
elegant	anggun
enthusiastic	peminat
essential / necessary / important	perlu / penting
evil	jahat
exciting	menarik
flawless / perfect	sempurna
flexible	fleksibel
frequently	selalu
fresh	segar
friendly	peramah / baik
generous	murah hati
gentle	lembut
good	baik
great	baik
handsome	kacak, tampan
honest	jujur
humorous	kelakar
important	penting
impressive	mengkagumkan
independent	merdeka / berdikari
intelligent	pandai / bijak
interesting	menarik
kind / nice	baik hati
lovely	indah

loyal	setia
lucky	bernasib baik
memorable	kenangan
neat	kemas
open minded	fikiran terbuka
ordinary / normal	biasa
patient	kesabaran
peaceful	aman
polite	bersopan
popular	mashyur / hebat / disukai ramai
positive	positif
powerful	berkuasa
precise	jitu
proud	bangga
reliable	boleh dipercayai
sane	siuman
sensitive	sensitif
sexy	seksi
smart / clever	bijak / pandai
solid	pejal
special	istimewa
strong	kuat
sturdy	kukuh
stylish	bergaya
sympathetic	bersimpati
tranquil	tenang
unforgettable	tidak dapat dilupai
useful	berguna
wise	bijaksana

NEGATIVE DESCRIPTIONS	GAMBARAN NEGATIF
annoying	mengganggu
awful	teruk

bad	tidak baik / buruk
impolite	kurang sopan
rowdy	suka bergaduh
careless	cuai / lalai
clumsy	kekok
corrupt	rosak
coward	pengecut
decayed (food , dead)	reput
disgusting	menjijikkan
horrible	mengerikan
idiot	bodoh
illiterate	buta huruf
isolated	terasing
jealous (love/ feelings)	cemburu / dengki
jealous / envy (work / person)	dengki / iri hati
lazy	malas
liar	wild
meaningless	tiada makna
nasty	kasar / jahat
obscene	lucah
quarrelsome	suka bergaduh
rude	tidak bersopan / biadab
ruthless	zalim
selfish	mementingkan diri
senseless	tiada perasaan
shame	malu
shameful	rasa malu
shameless	tidak malu
strange	ganjil
stupid	bodoh
taboo / obscene	pantang / lucah
unclear	tidak jelas
unacceptable	tidak boleh diterima

undesirable	tidak diingini
unlucky	kurang bernasib
unnecessary	tidak perlu
untidy (place)	tidak kemas (tempat)
unusual / unfamiliar	tidak biasa / tidak dikenali
wasteful	bazir
weak	lemah
worthless / futile	tidak bernilai / sia-sia

BAD BEHAVIOUR	KELAKUAN BURUK
dishonest	tidak jujur
harassment	gangguan
insult	menghina
Do not smoke here.	Jangan merokok di sini.
Do not stare so long.	Jangan merenung lama sangat.
Don't gossip.	Jangan mengumpat.
Don't touch me.	Jangan sentuh saya.
Is he stalking me?	Adakah dia mengekori saya?
Leave me alone.	Jangan pedulikan saya.
No. (I don't want.)	Tidak. (Saya tidak mahu)
Shut up	Diam.
Stop it.	Berhenti.
That is not fair.	Itu tidak adil.
Thief!	Pencuri!
What are you looking at?	Apa yang kamu pandang?
You are lying.	Kamu tipu.
You are rude.	Kamu tidak sopan.

COMPARISON	PERBANDINGAN
easy / light	mudah / ringan
difficult / heavy	sukar / berat / membebankan
bigger than	lebih besar daripada

smaller than	lebih kecil daripada
high	tinggi
medium	pertengahan / sederhana
low	rendah
alike	agak sama
as much/ as many	sebanyak / seramai
different	berbeza
even / equal	sama rata
identical	serupa
large / big	besar
main	utama
mainly	terutamanya
majority	kebanyakan
many	banyak / ramai
massive	besar
opposite / reverse	lawan
similar	sama seperti
the same	sama dengan

COMMANDS / IMPERATIVE PHRASES	ARAHAN / FRASA IMPERATIF
Be careful	Tolong berjaga-jaga
Be happy	Bergembiralah
Be quiet. (shut up)	Tolong diam. (Diam)
Bring it to me.	Tolong bawa ke sini.
Calm down!	Bertenang!
Cancel it.	Tolong batalkan.
Catch / hold.	Tangkap / Pegang
Close the door.	Tolong tutup pintu.
Come.	Mari.
Come in / Enter.	Sila masuk
Drink.	Minum
Do it.	Buatlah
Don't disturb.	Jangan ganggu

Don't ask me.	Jangan tanya saya
Don't be late.	Jangan lambat , ya.
Don't cry.	Jangan menangis
Don't forget.	Jangan lupa, ya.
Don't give up.	Jangan putus asa.
Don't lose it.	Jangan hilangkan ini.
Eat.	Makan
Follow me.	Ikut saya.
Get it.	Dapatkannya
Get out.	Keluar!
Get up.	Bangun
Give her.	Berikan kepadanya.
Give him.	Berikan kepadanya.
Give me.	Berikan kepada saya.
Go. / Leave.	Pergi
Guess.	Teka
Help me.	Tolong saya / Bantu saya
Hurry.	Cepat.
Knock on the door.	Ketuk pintu.
Lay down.	Tolong baring
Leave it alone.	Biarkan sahaja.
Let's go.	Mari kita pergi
Let's go. (slang)	Jom!
Let's wait.	Mari kita tunggu.
Listen to me.	Dengar cakap saya.
Listen.	Dengar.
Lock the door.	Kunci pintu.
Look.	Tengok.
Move.	Gerak.
Open the door.	Buka pintu.
Pay attention.	Minta perhatian
Pick it up.	Ambil ini
Please leave.	Tolong beredar / pergi.

Proceed / Go ahead.	Teruskan
Put it there.	Letak di sana.
Put on____.	Pakai _____.
Read it.	Bacalah.
Repeat after me.	Ulang selepas saya.
Run!	Lari!
Show me.	Tunjukkan pada saya.
Shut it off.	Tolong tutupkan.
Sit down.	Sila duduk.
Sleep.	Tidur
Take off (remove)____.	Tanggalkan _____.
Taste it.	Cuba rasa.
Tell me.	Beritahu saya.
Think about it.	Fikirkan tentang ini.
Trust / Believe me.	Percayalah saya.
Try it.	Cuba ini.
Turn on (the lights).	Pasang (lampu).
Wait.	Tunggu.
Wake up.	Bangun.
Write it.	Tuliskan.

ADVERB	SIFAT KATA / ADVERBA
accidentally	tidak sengaja
as	sebagaimana / seperti
approximately	lebih kurang / kira-kira
barely	hampir
basically	asasnya
carefully	berhati-hati
easily	senang-senang
exactly	tepat sekali
finally	akhirnya
generally	umumnya
honestly / really / truthfully	sejujurnya / sebenarnya / seikhlasnya

however	walau bagaimanapun
individually / separately	berasingan
jointly / together	sama-sama / bersama
lately	kini / akhir-akhir ini
luckily / by luck / by chance	nasib baik
mainly / especially	terutamanya
more than / extremely	lebih daripada
obviously	nyata / jelas
precisely / perfectly	dengan jitu
primarily / mostly	asasnya / kebanyakannya
quickly	cepat-cepat
repeatedly	berulang kali
sadly	malangnya / dukacitanya
slightly	sedikit
suddenly	tiba-tiba
surprisingly	terkejutnya
surely / certainly	tentunya
thankfully	bersyukur
unfortunately	tidak bernasib / malangnya
unlikely	tidak seperti

NON-CATEGORIZED WORDS

about	mengenai
about / nearly / almost	hampir
absent	tidak hadir
accomplishment	pencapaian
action	tindakan
activity	aktiviti
additional / supplementary	tambahan
advertisement / notice	iklan / pegumuman
advice / consultancy	nasihat / perundingan
affair / issue	hal / isu
aggressive	kasar
alien (being)	makhluk asing

alien (foreign)	asing
alternative	alternatif / pilihan
although	walaupun
anything	apa-apa
applicant	calon
appointment	temu janjii
appreciation / admiration	penghargaan / kekaguman
art	seni
at random	rambang
basket	bakul
because / reason	kerana / alasan
benefit	kebaikan
breast feeding	menyusu
bundle	ikatan
busy	sibuk
by the way	dengan itu
ceremony	upacara
chance / luck	peluang / nasib
change / transformation	transformasi
characteristic	ciri-ciri
chart / figure/ diagram	carta / gambar rajah
cheating	penipuan
collection	kutipan
combination	pergabungan
common	biasa
comparison	perbandingan
complicated / complex	kompleks
compliment	pujian
compromise	kompromi
concept	konsep
concern	khuatir
conclusion	kesimpulan
connection	perhubungan
consequence	kesan /implikasi

contribution	sumbangan
conversation	percakapan
copy	tiru
correction	pembetulan
creation / innovation	innovasi
criteria	kriteria
criticism	kritikan
data	data
deadline	tarikh akhir
deal (verb)	berurusan
deal (noun)	perjanjian
decision	pilihan
demonstration	demostrasi
dependent	bergantung kepada
design	rekaan
desire	kemahuan
destiny	takdir
detail / explanation	butir-butir
development	pembangunan
discovery	penemuan
distribution	pengedaran
division	bahagian
document	dokumen
doll	anak patung
drawing	lukisan
each	setiap
entrance	pintu masuk
equipment	alatan
established	telah mendirikan
estimate / guess	anggaran / tekaan
evaluation	penilaian
everybody	semua orang
everything	semua benda
example	contoh

exit	keluar
expectation	jangkaan
experience	pengalaman
expert	pakar
fair / fairness (just)	adil / keadilan
famous / known / popular	masyhur /terkenal / popular
fault	kesalahan
favor	mrmihsk
file	fail
final	terakhir
flexible (adjective)	anjal
for the future	untuk masa akan datang
forever	selama-lamanya / abadi
forgetfulness	kealpaan
former / prior	sebelum
fragile	rapuh
funding	pembiayaan
gigantic / huge	gergasi
goal / objective	tujuan / objektif
greed	ketamakan
guest / visitor	tetamu
hard work	kerja keras
headquarters	ibu pejabat
hero	pahlawan
hidden	tersembunyi
historic	bersejarah
hobby	hobi / kegemaran
hole / gap	lubang
illogical	tidak logik
influence	pengaruh
information	maklumat
interest	minat
intersection	persimpangan
item (thing)	benda

joke	gurau
junk	sampah
liar	wild
lie	tipu
light weight	ringan
livelihood	rezeki
logical	logik
lost	kehilangan
luxury	mewah
machine	mesin
match stick	mancis
meeting	mesyuarat
member	ahli
memory	peringatan
method	cara
mistake	kesalahan
mixture	campuran
model	model
mutual	bersama
not much	bukan banyak
nowhere	di mana-mana
nudity	berbogel
obedient	patuh
of course	tentulah
only	sahaja
opinion / idea	pendapat
opportunity / luck	peluang / nasib
original	asal
outward	luaran
overall	keseluruhan
paint / ink	cat /dakwat
painter	pengecat
pair / couple	pasangan
participation	penyertaan

partner	pasangan
patience	kesabaran
perception	persepsi / anggapan
performance	prestasi
permission / permit	kebenaran
perspective	perspektif / sudut pandangan
possible	boleh
possibly / maybe	mungkin
potential	keupayaan / potensi
precaution / warning	langkah berjaga-jaga
predication	benaran
preference	pilihan
presentation	persembahan
print	cetak
private	sendirian
process	proses
product	hasil
production	penghasilan / produksi
progress	kemajuan
progress / change	perubahan
project	projek
proposal	cadangan
purpose	tujuan / objektif
rare	jarang
ready	sedia
reality	kebenaran
record (file)	rekod
reflection	pantulan
regular / common	biasa
relief	legah
remainder	baki
report	laporan
reputation	reputasi
research	penyelidikan

reward	ganjaran
ripe / matured	matang / masak
row (horizontal line)	barisan
schedule	jadual
sculpture	ukiran
secret / mystery	rahsia / misteri
serious	serius
several (two, three)	beberapa
shadow / shade	bayang
shame	malu
sharp	tajam
shift / movement	anjakan / pergerakan
shiny	berkilau
shy	segan
situation / condition	keadaan
skill	kemahiran
stability	kestabilan
stack	timbunan
stationary	pegun
stick (verb)	melekat
stick (noun)	ranting
sting	sengat
storage	simpanan
stripes	belang
stuff	barangan
success	kejayaan
sufficient	mencukupi
support	sokongan
surroundings / environs	sekeliling / keadaan
system	sistem
talent	bakat
things	benda
thorough	menyeluruh
tolerable	diterima

tolerance	toleransi
toy	alat mainan
training	latihan
type	jenis
typical	biasa
unavailable	tiada
unavoidable	tidak boleh dijauhi
undeniable	tidak boleh dinafikan
universal	sejagat
until now	sehingga kini
varieties	kepelbagaian
various	berbagai
very	sangat
viewpoint	pandangan
visit	lawat
waste	sampah
wax	lilin
wealth / treasure	kekayaan
whatever	apa-apapun
widespread	tersebar luas

POPULAR EXPRESSIONS / SLANG

Following are expression, slang, and informal wording. Give them a try.

a friend	membe
As you wish!	Lantak.
Cannot.	Dok leh / Tak boleh.
Come here.	Mai.
cool, down to earth, awesome	sempoi
Don't!	Toksah!
Don't have.	Tak de.
Don't want.	Tak mau.
Don't know.	Tak tau.

Done (on work).	Beres
Go.	Pi
grandfather	wan
grandmother	tok
Hi friend, how are you?	Hai kawan, apa macam?
How are you, Uncle?	Pak, ada baikkah?
Is that so? / Really?	Ye ke?
I	Chek / gua
I love you	Gua cinta sama lu
Let's go.	Jom.
nice, well done, cute.	cun
none	Tak de, Tarak
not fair	Mana aci
Not tasty.	Dok dak
Ouch, it's painful!	Aduh, sakitnya!
really? / Is that so?	ye ka?
rickshaw	lanca
reverse (car)	gostan
What a pity!	Kesiannya!
Should not	Tak aci
stupid, silly	dungu
toilet	Jamban
you	lu / kau /depa
Where?	Kat mana?
Where?	Belah mana?

ANTONYMS	(LAWAN ERTI)
very	sangat
not very	tidak sangat
above	atas
below	bawah
ahead	hadapan

behind	belakang
already	sudah / selepas
not yet	belum
before	sebelum
after	selepas
first	pertama
last	akhir
forward	ke depan
backward	ke belakang
high	tinggi
low	rendah
in front	di hadapan
at the back	di belakang
inside	di dalam
outside	di luar
near	dekat
far	jauh
the next time	lain kali
the last time	masa lalu
to	kepada
from	daripada
up	atas
down	bawah
with	dengan
without	tanpa
awake	bangun
asleep	tidur
brave	berani / gagah
coward	pengecut
educated	berpendidikan
uneducated	tidak berpendidikan / buta huruf
funny	kelakar

serious	serius
fat	gemuk
thin	kurus
friendly	peramah
unfriendly	tidak ramah
happy	gembira
sad	sedih
male	lelaki
female	wanita (formal) / perempuan
married	berkahwin
single	bujang
modest	sederhana
arrogant	sombong / bongkak
polite	bersopan
rude	tidak bersopan / biadab
rich	kaya
poor	miskin / papar
shy	malu
sociable	peramah
sick	sakit / uzur
healthy	sihat
similar	sama
opposite	belawanan
smart	bijak
stupid	bodoh
strong	kuat
weak	lemah
success	berjaya
failure	gagal
tall	tinggi
short	pendek / rendah
thin	nipis
thick	tebal

wise	bijaksana
foolish	kebodohan
safe	selamat
dangerous	bahaya
easy	senang
difficult	sukar / susah
organized	terancang / teratur
disorganized	tidak terancang / tidak teratur.
interesting	menarik
boring	membosankan
true	benar / betul
false	salah / tidak benar
right	kanan
left	kiri
correct / right	betul
incorrect / wrong	tidak betul / salah
I am satisfied.	Saya berpuas hati.
I am not satisfied.	Saya tidak berpuas hati.
I understand	Saya faham.
I don't understand	Saya tidak faham.
famous (known)	terkenal
unknown	tidak diketahui
simple	mudah
complicated	rumit
tight	tegang (string) / ketat (apparel)
loose	longgar
smooth	licin
rough	kasar
straight	lurus
crooked	bengkok
loud	bising
quiet	sunyi
hot	panas

cold	sejuk
flat	datar / pamah
hilly / mountainous	berbukit / bergunung
ordinary	biasa
rare	jarang
full	penuh
empty	kosong
normal	biasa
abnormal	tidak biasa
exact	tepat
inexact	kurang tepat
beautiful (m/f)	segak / cantik
ugly	hodoh
early	awal
late	lambat
dry	kering / kontang
wet	basah
busy	sibuk
not busy	tidak sibuk
on	terpasang
off	tertutup
finished / completed	habis / selesai
unfinished/ incomplete	belum habis / belum selesai
still	tidak bergerak
moving	bergerak
permanent	kekal / abadi
temporary	sementara
expected	jangkaan
unexpected	tidak dijangka
better	lebih baik
worse	lebih buruk
large / big	besar
small / little	kecil

natural	semulajadi
man-made / imitation	buatan manusia / tiruan
edible	boleh dimakan
non-edible	tidak boleh dimakan
modern	moden
traditional	tradisional
important	mustahak / penting
unimportant	tidak mustahak / tidak penting
clean	bersih
dirty	kotor
foreign	asing
domestic	tempatan / domestik
efficient	cekap
inefficient	tidak cekap
comfortable	selesa
uncomfortable	tidak selesa
young	muda
old	tua
quick / fast	cepat / laju
slow	perlahan
working	bekerja (v) / berfungsi (machinery)
not working	tidak bekerja / tidak berfungsi
complete	selesai
incomplete	belum selesai
cheap	murah
expensive	mahal
dead	mati
alive	hidup
sure	tentu
unsure	tidak tentu
public	awam
private	swasta
deep	dalam

shallow	cetek
relaxing	berehat
stressful	bertekanan
similar	sama
different	berbeza
legal	sah
illegal	tidak sah
lucky	bernasib baik
unlucky	tidak bernasib baik / kurang bernasib
major	utama
minor	kecil
functional	berfungsi
dysfunctional	tidak berfungsi
convenient	sesuai
inconvenient	tidak sesuai
basic	asas
complex	rumit / kompleks
possible	berkemungkinan
impossible	tidak berkemungkinan
responsible	bertanggungjawab
irresponsible	tidak bertanggungjawab
real	benar
fake	palsu
vertical	menegak
horizontal	mendatar
visible	kelihatan
invisible	ghaib / tidak kelihatan
balanced	seimbang
imbalanced	tidak seimbang
useful	berguna
useless	tidak berguna
sharp	tajam

blunt	tumpul
timid	penakut
bold	berani
young / younger	lebih muda
old / older	lebih tua
exterior	luaran
interior	dalaman
hard	keras
soft	lembut
tolerant	tahan
intolerant	tidak bertahan
truthful	benar
dishonest	tidak jujur
entrance	masuk
exit	keluar
start	mula
finish	penamat
problem	masalah
solution	penyelesaian
minimum	minima
maximum	maksima
first name	nama pertama
last name (sur name)	nama keluarga
night	malam
day	siang
sun rise	matahari terbit
sun set	matahari terbenam
love	cinta / sayang
hate	benci
war	perang
peace	aman
developing countries	negara membangun

developed country	negara maju
adult	dewasa
child	kanak-kanak
open (v)	buka
close (v)	tutup
increase (v)	bertambah
decrease (v)	berkurang
found (v)	terjumpa
lost (v)	hilang
win	menang
lose	kalah / tewas
give (v)	beri
take (v)	ambil
catch (v)	tangkap
throw (v)	lempar
build (v)	bina
destroy (v)	binasa
send (v)	hantar
receive (v)	terima
join (v)	bersama
separate (v)	terpisah
push (v)	tolak
pull (v)	tarik
sit down	duduk
stand up	berdiri
pick it up	ambillah
put it down	letakkan
come (v)	mari
go (v)	pergi
combine (v)	campurkan / cantumkan
separate (v)	pisahkan
remember (v)	ingat

forget (v)	lupa

MALAY VERBS

Following is a list of hundreds of Malay verbs. Remembember, each verb is spoken the same way regardless of the personal pronoun, and regardless of past or present tense.

ENGLISH VERB	MALAY VERB (KATA KERJA)
absorb	menyerap
accept / receive / take	menerima
accompany	menemani
accomplish	memenuhi
accuse	menuduh
acquire	mendapat
adapt	membiasakan
add / increase	menambah
adjust	menyesuaikan
admire	mengagumi
advise / consult	menasihati
affirm / prove	mengesahkan (sah)
agree	bersetuju
aim	bertujuan
allow / permit	membolehkan
alter	mengubah
amaze	memukau / megagumkan
amputate	memotong
amuse	menghiburkan
analyze	menganalisis
annoy	menyakitkan hati
applause / clap	bertepuk
appreciate	menghargai
approach / be near	menghampiri
approve / permit	membenarkan
argue	berhujah
arrange	menyusun

arrest	menangkap
arrive	tiba
ask	bertanya
assemble	berhimpun
assess	menilai
assign	menugaskan (tugas)
assist	membantu
attach	melampirkan
attack	menyerang
attempt (try)	mencuba
avoid / inhibit	mengelakkan
bake	membakar
bathe	mandi
be (become)	menjadi
be able	dapat
be better	menjadi lebih baik
be born	dilahirkan
be busy	menjadi sibuk
be called	dipanggil
be found	dijumpai
be full / satisfied	berpuas hati
be happy	gembira
be healthy / heal	sihat / sembuh
be hungry	menjadi lapar
be ill	jatuh sakit
be jealous	dicemburui
be known	dikenali
be located	terletak
be moving / shaking	bergegar
be next	bersebelahan
be present	hadir
be sick	sakit
be sorry / sad	bersedih
be stressed	tertekan
be suitable	bersesuaian

be taller / extend	menjadi lebih tinggi/panjang
be thirsty	dahaga
be tired	letih
be unable tofind	tidak dapat cari
be useful	berguna
be younger/ be less	menjadi lebih muda
be / become / happen	menjadi
be amazed / surprised	terkejut
be angry	marah
beat	pukul
beautify / decorate	menghiasi
become good / successful	menjadi baik / berjaya
beg	mengemis
believe	percayai
bite	menggigit
blame	menyalahkan (salah)
bleed	berdarah
bless	memberkati
blow / pump	meniup
boil	mendidih
borrow	pinjam
bother	mengganggu
break	memecahkan
bring	membawa
brush	menggosok
build / construct	membina
burn	membakar
buy	membeli
calculate	megira (kira)
call (by phone)	menelefon
cancel	membatalkan
capture	tertangkap
carry	membawa
catch	menangkap
cease / halt	berhenti

celebrate	meraikan
change	bertukar
change money	menukar mata wang
chase	mengejar (kejar)
chat	bercakap (cakap)
cheat / trick / deceive	menipu (tipu)
chew	mengunyah (kunyah)
choose	memilih (pilih)
chop / cut	memotong (potong)
circle / orbit	mengelilingi (keliling)
clap	bertepuk
clarify	menjelaskan
clean	membersihkan
close / shut	menutup (tutup)
collect	memungut (pungut)
combine / mix	mencampurkan
come	datang
come back / return	pulang
complain	mengadu
comply	mematuhi
conceal / hide	menyembunyikan
conceive	hamil
connect	menyambung (sambung)
conserve / protect	memelihara
console	memujuk
contact	menghubungi
continue	bersambung
control	mengawal (kawal)
cook	memasak
correct	membetulkan
cough	batuk
count	mengira (kira)
cover / cap / wear	memakai
cover / conceal	menutup
create	mencipta

cross	melintas
cry / weep	menangis
cure	menyembuhkan
cut	memotong (potong)
dance	menari
decide / determine	menentukan
deforest	menerokai
delete	memadamkan
deny	menafikan
depend	bergantung
describe	menggambarkan
destroy (to)	(untuk) membinasakan
die	meninggal dunia
dig	menggali
disagree	membantah
disappear	ghaib
disappoint	mengecewakan
dislike	tidak menyukai
dismiss / expel / remove	menolak
disobey / refuse	menderhaka / menolak
dispose	melupuskan
distribute	mengedarkan
divide	membahagikan
do	membuat
drain	menyalirkan
draw	melukis
dream (during sleep)	bermimpi
dress	memakai
drink	minum
drive	memandu
drown	lemas
dry up	kering
eat	makan
edit	menyunting
elect	mengundi

embarrass	memalukan
embrace	memeluk
encourage	menggalakkan
endure	bertahan
enjoy	menikmati
enter	masuk
erase	memadamkan
err / to be wrong	bersalah
escape	melarikan diri
escape / runaway	melarikan diri
establish / found	menubuhkan
evaluate	menilai
examine	memeriksa
exceed	melebihi
exceed / surpass	melebihi
exchange	menukar
exit	keluar
explain	menerangkan
explode	meletup
fail / fall down	gagal
farm / plough	membajak
fear	takut
feed	memberi makan
feel	berasa
fight	berlawan
fill	memenuhi
find / get	mencari
find / earn	mendapat
finish	selesai
fix / repair	memperbaiki
flee	melarikan diri
flow	megalir
fly	terbang
follow up / chase / track down	mengejar (kejar)
force / compel	memaksa

forget	lupa
forget / neglect	mengabaikan
forgive	memaafkan
frighten	menakutkan
fry	menggoreng
gain / increase	bertambah
get	mendapat
get in / get on	memasuki / keluar
get off	turun
give	memberi
give back / return (a thing)	mengembalikan / memulangkan
give birth	melahirkan
go (depart)	bertolak
go out	keluar
gossip	mengumpat
govern	mentadbir
graze	meragut
greet	menyapa
grieve	bersedih
grind	mengisar
grow	menanam
grow old	menjadi tua
grow up / raise	membesar
growl	menggeram / menguam
guard / protect	melindungi
guess	meneka
haggle / negotiate price	menawar harga
hang	menggantung
hangout	melepak
harass	mengganggu
harm / injure	mencederakan
harvest	menuai
hate	membenci
have	mempunyai
have sex	bersetubuh

hear	mendengar
help	membantu
hide	menyorok
hire	menyewa
hit	memukul
hold	memegang
hug	memeluk
hunt	memburu
hurry	mempercepatkan
hurt	mencederakan
imagine	membayangkan
immigrate	berhijrah
immunize	mengimunisasikan
impale	menyula /menusuk
impede / hamper	menghalang
imply / suggest	mencadangkan
improve	memperbaiki
include	termasuk
infect	dijangkiti
influence	mempengaruhi
ingest	menelan
inherit	mewarisi
inquire / ask	bertanya
inspect	memeriksa
inspire / motivate	mengilhamkan
insult	menghina
intend	berhasrat
interrupt	mengganggu
intimidate	menakut-nakuti
introduce (people to eachother)	memperkenalkan
invite	menjemput
joke	bergurau
jump	melompat
keep	menyimpan
kick	menendang

kill	membunuh
kiss	mencium
knock	mengetuk
know / recognize	mengenali
laugh	ketawa
launder / wash clothes	membasuh
lay (something down)	meletakkan
lead	mengetuai
leak	kebocoran
learn	mempelajari
leave	meninggalkan
leave / quit	berhenti
lend	pinjam
lessen	mengurangkan
lick	menjilat
lie (lie down)	berbaring
lie (telling a lie)	berbohong
lift up / raise	mengangkat
like / love	menyukai
limp	tempang
listen	mendengar
live (to be alive/in a place)	hidup
to be available	terdapat
loan / lend (consumables)	meminjam
loan / lend (temporarily)	meminjam
lock	mengunci
look / see	memandang
lose (game / war etc)	kalah
lose (possession)	hilang
love	mencintai
lower / bring down	menurunkan
magnify / increase	membesarkan
make	membuat
make	melakukan
make better	memperbaiki

make fertile	meyuburkan
manufacture / produce	menghasilkan
marry	berkahwin
measure / weigh	menimbang
meet (a person, or at a place)	bertemu
meet / encounter	bermuka dengan
memorize	menghafal
milk	menyusui
mimic	meniru
miss (a bus / a class / etc)	ketinggalan
mix	mencampur
moan / groan	merintih
mourn	berkabung
move	bergerak
multiply	berganda
need	memerlukan
nominate	memilih
notice / notify	memberitahu
obey	mematuhi
offend	menyinggung perasaan
open	membuka
oppress	menindas
optimize	mengoptimumkan
organize	merancang
own / possess	mempunyai
paint	mengecat
pass / pass by	melalui
pay	membayar
pee / urinate	membuang air kecil
peel	mengupas
pierce	menusuk
pile	bertimbun
plan / devise	merancang
plant	menanam
plant / erect / establish	mendirikan

play	bermain
plow/plough	membajak
pollute	mencemarkan
poop (defecate)	membuang air besar
pour	menuang
practise	berlatih
preach	berkhutbah
predict	meramal
prefer	lebih suka
prepare	menyediakan
pretend	berpura-pura
prevent / prohibit	menghalang
print	mencetak
profit	mendapat keuntungan
protest	membantah
pull	menarik
punch	menumbuk
punish	mendenda
push	menolak
put	meletak
quit /step down	berhenti
rain	hujan
read	membaca
realize	menyedari
receive	menerima
reduce / decrease	mengurangkan
regret	menyesal
relax	berehat
remain	berkekal
remember	mengingati
remind	mengingatkan
rent	menyewa
repair	membaiki
repeat	mengulang
replace	menggantikan

report	melaporkan
respect	menghormati
restrain	menghalang
ride	menunggang
ripen / mature / cook	masak
roast / grill	memanggang
rob	merompak
rot	mereput
run	berlari
satisfy	memuaskan
save / keep	menyimpan
saw	menggergaji
say	mengatakan
scoop	mengaut
scream / shriek	menjerit
search / seek	mencari
see	menjenguk
seem	kelihatan
sell	menjual
send	menghantar
send / mail	menghantar / mengirim
separate	memisahkan
serve	berkhidmat
sew	menjahit
share	berkongsi
sharpen	mengasah
shave	mencukur
shoot	menembak
shop	membeli-belah
show / indicate	menunjukkan
shut	menutup
sift	mengayak
sign	menandatangani
signify / mean	menandakan
sing	menyanyi

sit	duduk
slaughter	menyembelih
sleep	tidur
slip	tergelincir
smash / shatter / crush	pecah
smell	menghidu
smile / grin	senyum / senyuman
snatch	menculik
soak	merendam
sow (plant)	menyemai
sow seed / scatter	menyemai
speak	bertutur
spend the day	menghabiskan siang hari
spend the evening	menghabiskan petang
spend the night	menghabiskan malam
spit	berludah
squeeze	memicit
stand	berdiri
stay	tinggal
steal	mencuri
step down	melangkah ke bawah
step on / tread on	melangkah ke hadapan
sting	menyengat
stir	mengacau
study	belajar
stumble	tersandung
subtract / discount	tolak
succeed	berjaya
suffer	menderita
suffice / be enough	mencukupi
supply	membekalkan
support	menyokong
surprise	terkejut
surround	dikelilingi
suspect	mengesyaki

swallow	menelan
sweat	berpeluh
sweep	menyapu
sweeten	memaniskan
swim	berenang
take	mengambil
take (someone's somewhere)	menemankan
take a picture	menangkap gambar
take care	menjaga diri
talk / speak	bercakap
taste	merasa
teach	mengajar
tear	mengoyakkan
tell	memberitahu
thank / praise	berterima kasih
think	berfikir
think of	memikirkan
threaten	mengancam
throw	membuang / membaling
tie / bind / imprison	mengikat
till (plough)	menbajak
to miss (an item)	terlepas
touch	menyentuh
trade	berdagang
translate	menterjemah
travel	melancong
treat a patient	merawat pesakit
trust	mempercayai
try	mencuba
turn (in direction)	pusing ke
turn (something)	memusing
turnover / peddle	mengayuh
understand	memahami
untie	membuka ikatan
update	mengemaskini

uproot	menumbangkan
use	menggunakan
visit	melawat
vomit	muntah
vote	mengundi
wait	menunggu
wake (someone) up	mengejutkan
wake up / get up	bangun
wakeup / be startled	bangun / terkejut
walk	berjalan
want	mahu / hendak
warn	memberi amaran
wash	memcuci
waste	membazirkan
wear	memakai
weed	merumput
welcome	mengalu-alukan
wet	membasahkan
whistle	bersiul
win (defeat)	kalah
wipe / rub clean	mengesat
wonder	tertanya-tanya
work	bekerja
worry	risau
write	menulis
yawn	menguap

About the writers:

The author, **Mae Cheong** is from Perak, Malaysia. Born and raised in Ipoh, a once famous tin mining city well known to the region. She received her primary and secondary school education in the national schools. She went to pursue a Ceritficate in Food Processing Technology in Kuantan, Pahang, and lately has graduated from her Degree in BA (Hons) in Liberal Studies.

She had worked in the food and water laboratories earlier in her career. She left her career and continues to work as a freelance tutor and in Science, Mathematics. English and Bahasa Melayu.

The editor, **Andrew Tadross** is a landscape architect, university lecturer, and co-author of *The Essential Guide to Tigrinya*, *The Essential Guide to Amharic*, and *Afan Oromo*. He visited Malaysia in 2014, and fell in love with the food and culture.

Mae Cheong and Andrew Tadross in 2014,
while visiting the Cameron Highlands

If you have found this book useful, we would sincerely appreciate a review on **Amazon.com.**

Terima kasih!!

Made in the USA
Middletown, DE
16 October 2023

40947311R00096